HISTORIC
MODEL SHIPS
from
SCRATCH

Nexus Special Interests Ltd.
Nexus House
Azalea Drive
Swanley
Kent BR8 8HU

First published by Nexus Special Interests Ltd., 1998

ISBN 1-85486-187-5

Front and back cover photos: Tom Reeves of Lewes, Sussex

Typeset by Kate Williams, Abergavenny.

Printed and bound in Great Britain by
Marston Book Services Ltd, Oxfordshire

HISTORIC MODEL SHIPS from SCRATCH

Scott Robertson

Nexus Special Interests

Contents

Acknowledgements

My grateful thanks are due to the following:

Brian Moseley for the paddle steamer drawings of
Compton Castle (Chapter 7).
Dr Philip L Armitage, the curator of Brixham
Museum & Historical Society, for his help with the
Brixham trawler drawings (Chapter 14).
Harvey's Brewery of Lewes for the picture of the old
barge *Centaur* (page 23).

My special thanks go to **Susan Knutsen** of Lewes for
her excellent photographs covering the *Golden Hind*
(pages 107 and 108) during a visit to Brighton in
1996.

Foreword

One of the problems of writing about a craft subject as detailed as model ships is what to include and what to leave out in order to stimulate interest without boring the reader.

A new enthusiast to the hobby needs to know how to understand the makings from nothing using raw materials. It is more than likely that he or she is moving on from the already prepared kit method of the craft.

My first book, *Model Ships from Scratch* (1994, Nexus Special Interests) assumed that the reader wanted a crash course on this interesting subject.

The historical periods covered were wide to tempt you into whatever period you might find interesting.

In this new book I go deeper into this fascinating hobby and try to answer some of the problems, enlarge upon the subjects covered before and introduce new branches of the craft. I will also touch on some of the more unusual methods of model ship making.

The same old truisms apply – it is an inexpensive hobby, the tools you will need are few, the patience you will need is infinite and the end results can be spectacular.

Introduction

Ship models have been constructed from earliest times. The Egyptians put model rowing and sailing craft into the tombs of nobles as symbols of great earthly possessions to be carried over into the next world. In Cornwall, Eire and Guernsey, they figured in a primitive rite on Good Friday when every fisherboy, following tradition, sailed his model boat to herald in the new fishing season. In Spain, models of local ships were hung up in the church to ward off disasters that were all too common in historical times.

French prisoners-of-war have left behind magnificent model ships made from whalebone, mutton bone and human-hair rigged ships. Long sea journeys have also spurred on bored sailors into producing good models of their ships. Although these are interesting facts, I am sure that most readers will be making their model ships for no other reason than sheer pleasure.

Moving on now into deeper water to try to tackle more problems about hull construction, rigging and deck detailing. Model ships in bottles are featured together with half-block models and nautical dioramas.

I have received many letters from readers of *Model Ships from Scratch*. The hobby is obviously a worldwide pursuit – Australia, South Africa, France, America and other countries all feature in my mail. In this new book I hope that enthusiasts who have not fallen at the first hurdle will enjoy this further excursion into model ship construction. Judging by the pictures that are enclosed in the letters I receive of models completed by readers, which are both superb and very encouraging, it must be working – so keep modelling!

Author's note

Although every effort has been made to present entirely new material in this book, some subjects covered in *Model Ships from Scratch* inevitably appear in part, but with additional drawings and information. Where possible, the plan numbers are quoted from the Nexus Special Interests Plans Service. The *Plans Handbook* (published by Nexus) is a handy publication which contains over 500 plans of both old and modern vessels.

1 Ships in bottles

You may raise an eyebrow to find this subject included here, but it makes a real change as a modeller of old ships to miniaturize your efforts and then preserve them in a bottle. They make great gifts and are completed quite quickly.

The mass production of bottles in the 1800s, of various useful shapes, seems to have increased the sailors' interest in putting little model ships into bottles. Before then hand-blown upright carafes were used, not only for early crude models of ships but scenes of the Crucifixion, street scenes, chapels and altars and other subjects of interest to sailors on long boring sea journeys.

How much easier it is for us today, as landlubbers with a nice workshop or kitchen table. No pitching hideaway on a ship with coarse materials to work with for us. Believe me, it's not difficult to make a small model that ends up looking good in a discarded whisky or gin bottle – a lot of the fun is in disposing of the contents beforehand!

The tools you will need cost very little and you will certainly have most of them knocking about your workshop. Anything else you can make from old wire coathangers, snipped razor blades, cocktail sticks and small things from your junk box. This all sounds like a *Blue Peter* project but bear with me.

The tools

- Hobby knives or scalpel (with changeable blades)
- Scissors
- Wire snippers
- Tweezers
- Various homemade probes
- Cutting probes, various types, homemade
- Needles and pins
- Old wire coathangers
- Small pin vice
- Old darning needles

The old darning needles make good mini drill bits to use in a pin vice, or you can push one end into a short piece of dowel stick after applying superglue to this end. File or grind two or three flats

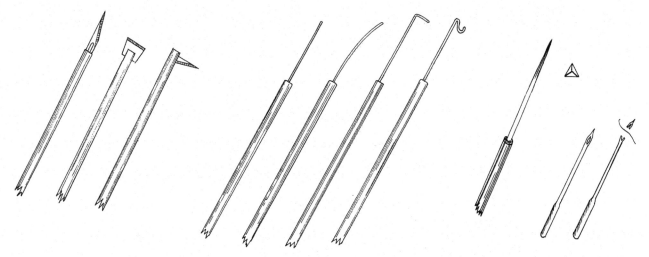

Fig 1.1 *Three types of probe cutters – a normal straight cutter, a forward cutter and a back cutter. Four types of stiff wire probes mounted on thin dowels and needle drill, sharpened on two or three sides at tip. Sewing machine needles with the point snapped off make good small drills. These needles come in all sizes.*

1

on the other end. It is also an idea to keep a needle on a long thin dowel stick for use, when heated red, to burn off unwanted cottons of rigging (to be explained later). See some of the above-mentioned illustrated.

The bottle

Obviously you will need a nice clear glass bottle. Whatever shape it is, the opening will need to be at least ¾" across the mouth – avoid any that choke a little in the neck. Choose a short-necked type for your first effort. To a large extent, the shape of the bottle will dictate the type of ship. Its mast height to hull length ratio will be a factor in choosing your model.

The dimple *Haig* whisky bottle is one of the most popular shapes, hence its relative scarcity – look out at car boot sales! Clear vodka bottles and *Plymouth* gin types are good. An upright model can be accommodated in a *Mateus Rosé* bottle and looks very novel. See **Fig 1.2** for suggested bottle shapes.

Procedure

Wash the bottle well in hot water and drain. Dry it neck down, having removed labels and any adhesive. Check for any streakiness inside and polish out with a slightly damp paper towel on a piece of wire coathanger. Check the casting seam – this must remain underneath your model. It may help at this stage, especially with round bottles, to have some kind of cradle to lay the bottle down on so that it will not roll off your work surface. See **Fig 1.3**.

The first thing to tackle is the sea in your bottle. At this stage, if you have never bottled a ship, the type of sea is likely to be the least thing on your mind, but it is important at this early stage. Various materials are used but avoid anything like plaster, *Polyfilla* or any water-based substance as these will sweat when sealed and you will never get rid of the moisture however well you dry it out beforehand. Wood, ordinary putty, plasticine and some types of

Fig 1.2 Different types of suitable clear glass bottles.

craft modelling clay are the most suitable for making the sea base for the model.

Assuming that you are using putty, roll small billets of the material into thin sausages, thread lengthways onto a kebab stick then thread into the neck of the bottle. Be careful not to touch the inside neck of the bottle and leave smudges. If you do, these marks can be removed with the paper towel on a wire probe. Push off the sea material with a secondary stick or wire. Press the material down onto your bottle's inside base with a piece of dowel or anything else that will comfortably go through the bottle neck.

When all this is done you will need a hull shape of your model, suitably fixed on a stiff probe, to make an impression where the ship model will eventually rest on the sea. Remember that the model hull will be a waterline model with a flat bottom. It is a good idea to use a blank piece of ⅛in. plywood of the same shape as the hull model bottom when making your slight indentation in the sea. Be careful

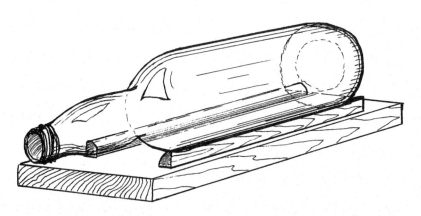

Fig 1.3 A simple bottle rest to keep round bottles in place while working.

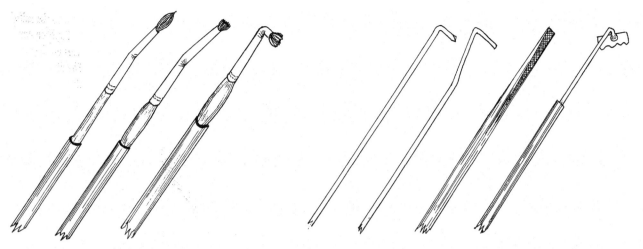

Fig 1.4 *Three types of brushes with the bristle holding ferrules slightly bent. This helps when painting the sea. Remember that the brushes have to go through the bottle neck charged with paint, so only a slight bend, or none at all. Four different types of probe tools (coathanger wire is used). Two types with right-angle tips, one sharpened chisel fashion. One wooden dowel sharpened screwdriver fashion and a blunt rake type, made by soldering a strip of thin sheet metal to wire piece. These will help mould the sea base.*

with this placement and allow for the bowsprit length. When this is done the sea texture can be fiddled with. I find that a thick wire with its end flattened a little and sharpened (chisel fashion) with this tip bent at right angles serves well to flick and mould the sea surface. See **Fig 1.4**.

Before tackling the details of your model the sea surface can be coloured, which will give time for it to dry properly.

Avoid thick gooey paint – model, oil or water-soluble paints are fine. Semi-matt and matt types are best. If you are using plasticine for the sea, blue, green and white are useful, either layered in the bottle or pre-mixed before putting in the bottle. If you have layered the three colours, score around with your probe tool on the bottom of the bottle for an artistic sea effect.

When painting the sea small brushes are used – 0 and 1, 2 and 3 sizes are best. You will soon find out by trial and error which are the most suitable. The brush's metal ferrule may have to be bent at a slight angle to the brush shaft, and the shaft made longer to get at the inside extremities of the sea base. You can practise a blend of colours on a stiff paper before attempting to paint inside the bottle, any paint that gets on the glass can be removed with the trusty paper towel on a wire probe. Ship wakes and bow wave can be scumbled in with your paintbrush. Avoid the brightest whites – go for a broken white. Tip lightly the white horses on the sea for an effective contrast. Try to remember the sea movement and tidal direction in relation to the hull when decorating the sea. Put aside to dry well.

The model

Virtually any type of wood can be utilized for the hull – pine, hardwood offcuts and even balsa wood if it is the harder variety. The type of ship I found

best to start with was a fore and aft sailer with one or two masts such as a cutter type or a Brixham trawler. Square riggers are a little more complicated to start with.

Before starting, push a flexible rule into your bottle and check the exact interior area. Remember the bowsprit and include it in the length required in your calculations. **Fig 1.5** best describes the different stages of shaping the hull. Fretsaw or hand carve the hull blank. Cut in any change of deck level and sheer as in some schooners, and fore and poop decks of square riggers.

Decking is best marked or scored on a separate strip of material. A thin morsel of veneer. A piece of brown paper suitably marked with a blunt needle or fine pen looks convincing as deck planking. Stick this down onto your deck area. See **Fig 1.5**.

Bulwarks around the deck edge can now be stuck on. The wood strip for this can be ⅟₃₂in. or ⅟₁₆in. thick – this all depends on scale. The bending can be done using a soldering iron. Rub the inside of strip as you ease in a curve and hold until cool. Bending using moisture is another way of bending. When ready these must be stuck on very well as these bulwarks will be drilled through for threading the rigging. Any wale thickening or rubbing strake can now be added.

Finally, sandpaper the hull. Colour the deck with wood sealer or any transparent medium you use. Paint the hull and bulwarks. If you have enough patience you may add a capping rail or poop rail – this kind of detail is up to you. Finish off the rest of deck detailing, cabins, rudders and hatches etc.

Setting up your model

You may, at this stage, fix your model hull down on a solid base to work on. I have a board with a few useful attachments and belaying points that I use

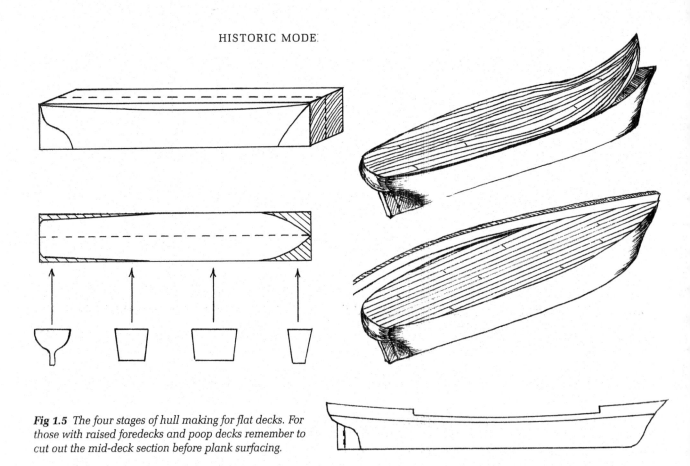

Fig 1.5 *The four stages of hull making for flat decks. For those with raised foredecks and poop decks remember to cut out the mid-deck section before plank surfacing.*

sometimes. See **Fig 1.6**. The beginner will certainly find this useful.

If your model has a bowsprit make sure the wood isn't too thin as you will be drilling through this. Glue the bowsprit in place.

Make your masts with suitable doubling well glued. You can mark in any mast caps or mast irons in black after painting or staining the masts. I have used slivers of pitch pine, cocktail sticks and kebab sticks for masts of this size. I coat the butt end of the mast in wood glue or instant glue. When hardened this prevents the mast butt splitting when it is drilled across for making the mast hinges. The mast hinges are made of brass wire, bent like a croquet arch after threading through the mast ends. See **Fig 1.7**. Drill the deck and push through, making

sure that the mast butt is not pressing onto the deck. If the wire is long enough to go right through to the underside of the hull, these small prongs form a good anchor in the sea base. This can be a nuisance when pushing the model into the bottle neck. You can decide to leave or snip off any spare wire.

At the base of the mast doubling, drill a hole. See **Fig 1.8**. This is to thread the two or three shrouds through. Take the shroud lines (cotton, thin rayon button cord or whatever you choose), knot one end then drill the belaying points along the edge of the bulwark, both sides. It is very important that these holes are all aft of the mast butt ends. See **Fig 1.9**. This makes sure that the mast will collapse. Thread through the bulwark all your knot-ended shroud lines from the inside of bulwark outwards. See

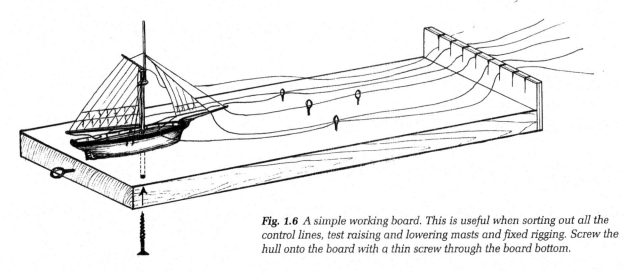

Fig. 1.6 *A simple working board. This is useful when sorting out all the control lines, test raising and lowering masts and fixed rigging. Screw the hull onto the board with a thin screw through the board bottom.*

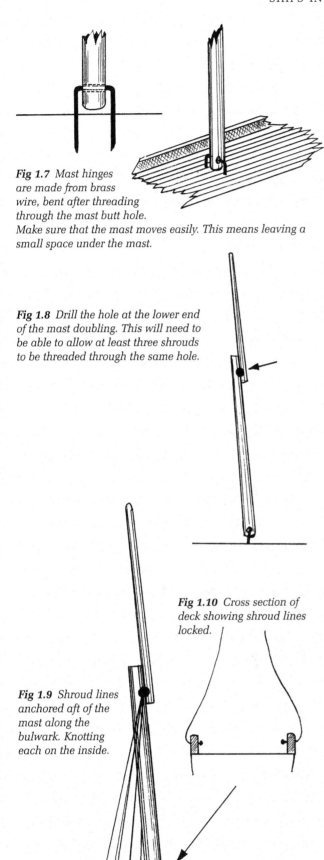

Fig 1.7 Mast hinges are made from brass wire, bent after threading through the mast butt hole. Make sure that the mast moves easily. This means leaving a small space under the mast.

Fig 1.8 Drill the hole at the lower end of the mast doubling. This will need to be able to allow at least three shrouds to be threaded through the same hole.

Fig 1.9 Shroud lines anchored aft of the mast along the bulwark. Knotting each on the inside.

Fig 1.10 Cross section of deck showing shroud lines locked.

Fig 1.10. Pull the shroud lines tight and thread them all through the mast hole at the doublings. Repeat the threading through the bulwarks on the other side and pull tight with the mast in its final erected position. A slight rake of the mast in its proper position should be aimed for. Place small drops of glue where the shrouds come through the holes to secure.

When positioned at the lower end of each shroud, little drops of thick paint of PVA glue assimilate deadeyes or bottlescrew shroud tensioners when dried and painted.

In most cases it is not possible to show ratlines on the shrouds, but you can try to assimilate a sheer pole just above the deadeye position. A whisker of cocktail stick will work here. When the sheer pole is fixed and dry, coat with thin glue or a little matt varnish. See **Figs 1.9** and **1.10**.

Gaffs and booms

If you fit sails to your model, the gaff spar and sail boom must be allowed a fair amount of flexibility, so make a running hinge for each at the mast end. See **Fig 1.12**. This control line is pulled up tight when the model is in the bottle.

If sails are not fitted you simply use the above system to hinge the booms and gaff to the mast permanently (see **Fig 1.11**) before bottling.

Sails

Thin paper, such as typing or writing paper (cream, offwhite or tan coloured) is used for the sails. Furled sails can be made from fine tissue paper, suitably bunched and tied. Tea or weak coffee colours work well.

The fixing of the sails to the two spars on a fore and aft model must be very secure. Use white types of glue to avoid staining the sails. Draw on sail detail lightly with pencil, not forgetting furling points and canvas seams. See **Fig 1.12**.

The spars can be glued directly to the sail edge. A more secure method is to carefully split the spars in half and glue half on each side of the sail edge. This can only be done if you have used strips of kebab or cocktail stick for the spars as they are made of a form of cane which splits well. Carefully colour the spars to avoid marking the sails.

The final set-up

You may have worked from a reduced plan, or even an off-the-cuff creation, but whichever reference you have used now is a good time to check every detail. Make sure all the holes are drilled nicely and that the running threads move easily through holes in the bowsprit, stern and prow.

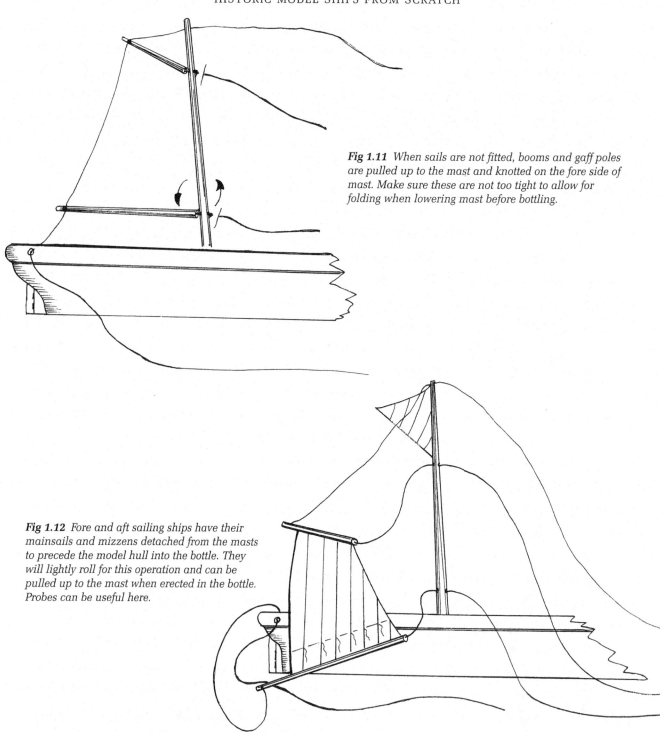

Fig 1.11 *When sails are not fitted, booms and gaff poles are pulled up to the mast and knotted on the fore side of mast. Make sure these are not too tight to allow for folding when lowering mast before bottling.*

Fig 1.12 *Fore and aft sailing ships have their mainsails and mizzens detached from the masts to precede the model hull into the bottle. They will lightly roll for this operation and can be pulled up to the mast when erected in the bottle. Probes can be useful here.*

Figs 1.13 & 14 *Two different ships in different shaped bottles. A malt whisky and a dimple Haig whisky bottle.*

Try a practice collapse of the model's mast etc. You can attach any flags required at this stage. A bit of gilt, perhaps on the prow, can be simulated from gilt chocolate paper or a touch of pale gilt model paint. An anchor, made of glue-stiffened cotton, can be added now.

Bottling your model without sails

The drawn illustrations show you at a glance how everything should look if you have got it right. If you have used a mounting board you will have quite a few control lines to deal with. Try to keep them in groups when you detach the model from the board. Check carefully inside the bottle that the sea colouring is dry – you don't want any smudges on the model.

A sail-less model should be no problem to bottle as the number of lines are few. Simply lower the mast and carefully manoeuvre the model into the bottle neck, stern first, making sure that your control lines remain outside the bottle. See **Figs 1.15, 1.16** and **1.17**.

When the model is just inside the bottle, try to lift it slightly with long-nosed tweezers to avoid any scraping of the sea. Place it in the indented sea surface and press lightly down. This should be enough to hold it, but just to make sure keep a little downward pressure while pulling very gently on the mast raising line and the forepeak brace lines, finishing with the main boom sheet line.

Check that the mast is upright with no sideways sag. Any lines not in immediate use can be belayed on the exterior of bottle neck. A rubber band around the neck or a spot of *Blu-Tack* will do this.

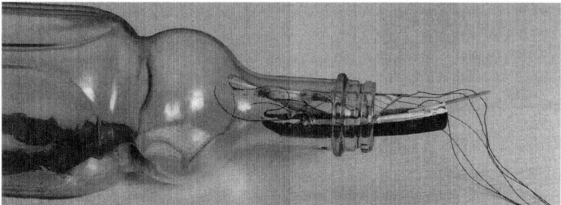

Figs 1.15, 16 & 17 The three stages of bottling a ship model. Check the masts fold and erect outside the bottle. Fold and push into bottle carefully. Firm the hull into the sea, then gently raise the masts.

Making all control lines fast permanently on the model is done one after the other. The mast fore brace first, ending with boom sheet line. Apply quick-drying adhesive by using one of your probes on the model's control lines where they are threaded through the various holes in the model and keep taut until dry. Check the shrouds are tight by keeping the mast line tight while drying.

Do not overdo the application of fast glue. Whatever it says on the tube it will keep in a wet state long enough for you to place a small drip where you want it.

When this is complete and thoroughly dry, take your cutting probes and cut off the control lines as close as possible, one at a time, pulling them out of the bottle as you go. Any stubs of control lines remaining can be burnt off with a red-hot needle probe – very carefully!

The model hull should be quite firm without having used any adhesive on its bottom. If you are a belt and braces type you can place a small amount of glue into the indentation before placing your model in the bottle.

Polish up the bottle and check for interior smudges and remove. I leave the model for about a week at an average room temperature before corking or capping.

Bottling your model with sails

Your first effort of a model with sails should be a single mast type – a fishing cutter or pilot ship is a good example.

If you try to push it all together through the bottle neck there will be tears. The idea is that some of the

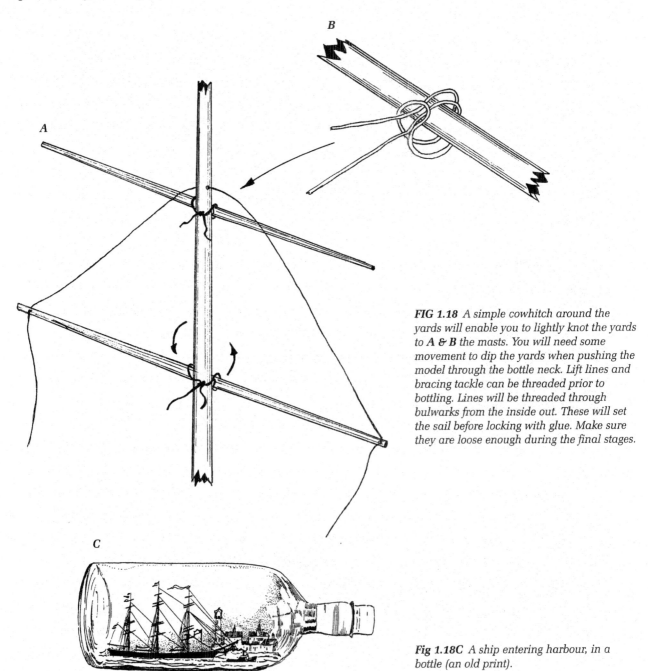

FIG 1.18 *A simple cowhitch around the yards will enable you to lightly knot the yards to **A & B** the masts. You will need some movement to dip the yards when pushing the model through the bottle neck. Lift lines and bracing tackle can be threaded prior to bottling. Lines will be threaded through bulwarks from the inside out. These will set the sail before locking with glue. Make sure they are loose enough during the final stages.*

Fig 1.18C *A ship entering harbour, in a bottle (an old print).*

sails can be rolled and pushed through first. They will still be connected to the mast by the control lines on the gaff and main sail boom. See **Fig 1.15**. The jib sails have their fore edge glued to the forestays. The foot of these sails or sail where the line comes away goes through a hole in the bowsprit, then becomes a control line.

With the mainsail gaff and boom rolled and pushed into the neck, follow with the hull and jib sails. With your probes, try to let the mainsail go to one side while positioning the hull. Then, when you are happy with this, start easing up the main mast. Lock with glue the mast lifting line as before when the mast is at correct position, followed by the jib lines. Pull the gaff and mainsail boom up to the mast with the two other lines. Pull any main boom sheet line to the correct degree of tack position you need

to show. Lock all the lines as you go and finish as described for the sail-less version of model.

Square-rigged models

These are a little more difficult. The square sail yards are attached to the masts (see **Fig 1.18A**). You can fit yard lifts and braces – a lot depends on the degree of detail you want featured in your model. Any fore and aft sails between masts and the mizzen are dealt with as described for the single mast type. All square sails are glued in position on the yards. Sail brace or tack lines must have slack in them for when the mast is down. See **Fig 1.18A**.

Sails will need a little shaping for wind effect. Roll cut-out sails around a thin dowel to curve the

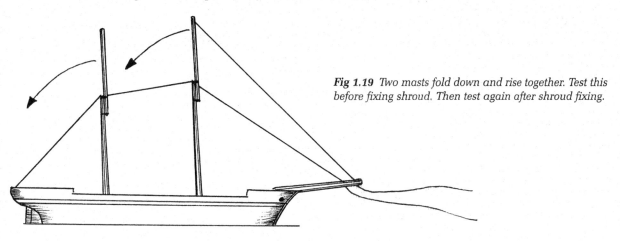

Fig 1.19 *Two masts fold down and rise together. Test this before fixing shroud. Then test again after shroud fixing.*

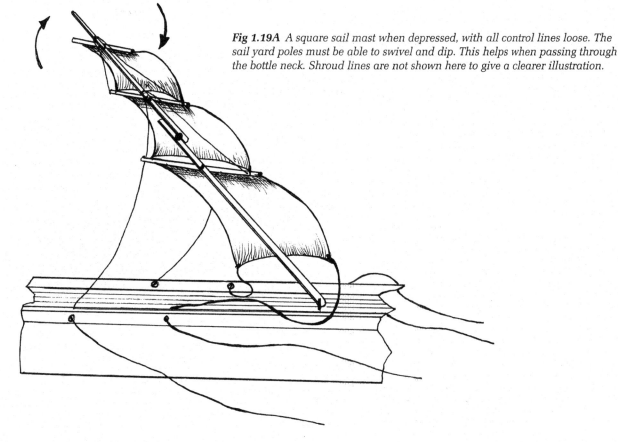

Fig 1.19A *A square sail mast when depressed, with all control lines loose. The sail yard poles must be able to swivel and dip. This helps when passing through the bottle neck. Shroud lines are not shown here to give a clearer illustration.*

square sails. Do this after you have pencilled in sail seams and reefing points etc.

Once you have successfully made a good job of models with single masts, try two and three mast models. You simply repeat what you did with one mast. The two or three masts will all erect at the same time as only one control line is used. See **Fig 1.19**. Make sure all yards are able to twist a little so that during bottling they can pass through the neck. Your various probes can straighten the yards and set sails when the model is set in the bottle.

Finishing off

You can make a stand for round- or flask-shaped bottles. Dimple *Haig* and *Johnny Walker* type whisky bottles will stand on their own, though a nice dark polished wood stand will finish off the project and afterwards you will probably feel like having a crack at those plans you have tucked away for the really big model ship.

This area of the model ship hobby is certainly not set in stone. You will, no doubt, find your own way once the general idea is understood.

Bottles are plentiful, although not always with a ¾in. hole at the mouth. Some are mineral tinged with a green cast. These are usable and look similar to the old antique bottles. If you really cannot be bothered see **Fig 1.20**.

As a footnote to these instructions it is worth mentioning that making sails from paper isn't necessarily the rule. If you can find some tightly woven material that you feel you can handle, use this. It will obviate the necessity to keep the fore mainsail and mizzen separate as in **Fig 1.12**. The only reason for this is to stop paper sails crumpling. With material you can hinge booms to the mast permanently before threading into the bottle as material is very resilient and reverts back to shape after raising the mast.

The marking in of canvas seams should be made with a sharp soft pencil as this avoids bleeding of colour into the material.

It is a good idea after you have cut out the sails to lightly edge with a brush and PVA glue – this prevents losing a thread or two while fitting sails to booms etc.

As mentioned in the introduction to this book, during the years between 1793 and 1815 some of the finest craftsmen included prisoners-of-war, with talents that were well beyond ours of today. Spanish, French, Dutch and American prisoners all featured in prison populations imprisoned in England. Places like Portsmouth, Devonport and Chatham all had prison hulks moored in their harbours. Various prisons – *Portchester Castle*, *Norman Cross*, *Peterborough*, *Taunton*, *Tonbridge* and *Perth* – housed these unfortunate sailors.

Earning money was very important to these men and there were many devious methods by which they could distribute the things they made to interested buyers. Some of these men came from honourable pursuits. Ivory carvers from Dieppe and West Africa, Breton jet carvers and French jewellers and watchmakers all found themselves pressganged into the Navy by a desperate Napoleon who was losing the war at sea.

Between 1812 and 1816, the years of the American war, large numbers of American seamen found themselves interned. A good number of these men were from whaling ships so 'scrimshaw' work and bone carving was something with which to pass the time. Some excellent bone models, mainly frigates, were made by these men. The French also made excellent model ships using bones from their rations and material scrounged from prison rubbish dumps.

One story of interest to modern model makers was that of the prisoner Germain Lamy and his friend at Forton Camp, Hampshire. They made a 74-gun ship measuring only six inches long and sold it for £40 (a lot of money in those days). When M. Lamy returned to France he had amassed a fortune from his models – 17,000 francs must have given him a good start in civvy street!

This information, although interesting, may seem irrelevant to readers but it does show that putting a ship in a bottle seems a fairly easy job after all.

Fig 1.20 *This is the bottle for the impatient model maker who gave up on the other types of bottles!*

2 A Trafalgar ship – its construction and other capital ships

If you want a challenge to build from scratch

The average ship modeller will not make many of these types of ships in his or her lifetime because the process can take quite a time, and in order to get all the interesting deck and mast details into it, the model has to be big – 3ft 6in to 4ft is not a kitchen-table project! A good set of plans can run to seven or eight sheets at £10 per sheet. A lot depends on your previous knowledge, skill and pocket, but you can get away with three sheets like the Harold A. Underhill plan (Bassett Lowke) that I used.

A 3rd Rater was a useful ship to the British Navy at the turn of the eighteenth century. Many took part at Trafalgar (1805) carrying between 74 to 80 guns of differing weights that included standard 32 lb cannons and carronades. I decided that to build up a hollow hull with frames and planks in the traditional fashion would end up with the project perhaps never being finished, so a half solid lower hull was decided upon to get the whole project started with some hope of finishing it. (See **Fig 2.1**)

The lower hull was made up of eight pieces of pine, the length of the hull. These were cramped and glued together giving a block a little over-size to cut down to the shape needed. Plan measurements were carefully noted for the different cross-section stations along the hull. The block was then reduced into shape with draw knife, plane, rasps and sand-paper. Measurement checks with templates cut from the plan details were used carefully throughout the shaping of the hull block. The lower part of the hull in craft of this period was round and barrel-shaped, the upper sides tumbling home. This higher hull wall was cut from ⅛in. plywood (cross-cut when acute bending was necessary).

Note: this mode of construction is described for a model frigate in *Model Ships from Scratch* pages 23, 24, 25 and 27.

Two extra blocks of wood are now needed profiled for the stern and bow to support the top deck. The bow piece is a must. You may choose not to use a stern piece, this being squared off before building out the stern swelling with windows. (See **Fig 2.2**)

The ply sides are now measured off the plan allowing just a little extra length to allow for the curve. Fret out the gun ports. The prow piece plywood must be cut on the cross to enable proper bending around the bluff-shaped bow. The large lower hull block can be rebated to receive the ply sides and prow walls, or small beading strips can be glued inside the top edge of the hull block to receive

Fig 2.1 *The lower hull block made up of eight pieces of pine. Carved and finished with top section of hull made of plywood added, including the top deck pierced in the centre section.*

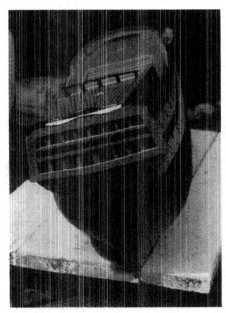

Fig 2.3 The main cabin windows built out over stern counter and hull sides. Thin transparent plastic stuck behind window main framing. Glazing bars carefully painted with No.1 brush on reverse side of glass.

Fig 2.2 The deck laid and bulwarks built up. Poop deck and steps finished. Deck drilled for three masts. Everything painted as you proceed.

the ply. **Fig 2.1**. The top deck is now marked out and cut to size out of ⅛in. ply, taking out the midship portion which is later beamed across to support the larger ships boats. **Fig 2.2**.This ply deck can be used as a support for your planking or ruling up directly onto the ply to assimilate planking if you choose to. Fix the top deck into the two sides of the hull, resting each end on bow block and stern piece if used – if not, use bead ledges glued inside the sides at the stern.

The poop deck can now be cut and fixed onto small strip beadings glued to the inside of the upper ply sides. Cut this deck very slightly over-size across the width, bend in when gluing. This gives a very slight curve to the deck.

The gunwales are thickened and built onto the inside with 1/16in. or 1/32in. ply, false timber heads first being glued into the hull to form a core for fixing. The cross section of the gunwale is tapered, thicker at the bottom, thinner at the top rail. Try to

Fig 2.4 Deck detailing half finished. Ships' boats hand-carved and set up with canvas covers over centre section beams. Some top deck cannons fitted with bracings etc. Stern davits, chainplates, anchor cats, bowsprit main timbers, figurehead and grating all fitted. Note: companion-way canvas shields fitted, opening side facing poop deck.

Fig 2.5 Close-up of poop deck with steering wheel fitted just under poop deck.

Fig 2.6 Masts pre-made and fitted, including main tops.

Fig 2.7 See masts fitted showing mast reinforcement timbers each side with iron mast bands, these made of gum strip built up around mast to correct thickness.

Fig 2.8 Close-up of steering position under poop deck, gratings and shot garlands. Small newel posts at top of each set of stairways for hand ropes.

Fig 2.9 Side view of hull showing chainplates. Although gun ports are closed they all have hinges that show.

Fig 2.10 Rigging started. Main braces and shrouds fitted.

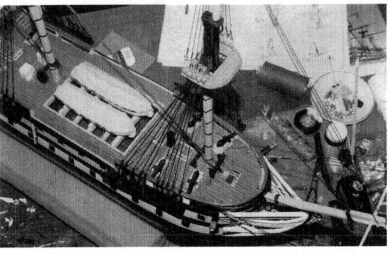

Fig 2.11 Mizzen shrouds with ratlines tied.

make sure that the false timber heads form the side frames of the gun ports. When lining the gunwales inside carry the cladding across the gun ports. When everything is glued and dried, cut down from the top of the gunwale and remove this area on each gun port along the gunwale. A thick top rail is fixed along the top to form the fourth side of the gun port. (See **Fig 2.8**)

The stern cabin area can now be built onto the stern area. **Fig 2.3**. The prow blade, keel piece and rudder post can be glued into position before fixing the stern cabin area or before you start on any deck detail.

The bowsprit is now drilled into the hull at the correct angle and the beakhead detail can be started.

As you will see from the progress pictures, deck furniture and detail is completed from the inside

Fig 2.12 Side view showing chainplate attachments to hull.

Fig 2.13 Finished stern windows, nameplate and stern chaser gun ports. Rudder still to be fitted.

Fig 2.14 General view of half-rigged model.

outwards. Mast drilling etc. is done early. The masts and tops are made completely before gluing into the hull (**Fig 2.7**) showing the masts fixed into the deck.

Painting as you proceed is very important as the detail gets denser on deck and the painting gets complicated if you don't.

When all main deck detail is finished you can glue and pin all the channel board chainplates etc. Ships' boats should, if possible, be carved out of the solid and fitted out. I used soft pine, but balsa wood is fine providing it is well painted and rubbed down between coats. (See **Fig 2.9**) I covered the two large midship boats with canvas tops to avoid a tricky carving job inside!

Fig 2.15 *Lower shrouds and ratlines tied and finished.*

Fig 2.17 *Ships' boat covers coloured black. Hammock nettings stowed with hammock bed rolls along centre section of deck.*

Fig 2.16 *Bow area with finished bowsprit rigging with flag and sprit boom in place.*

Fig 2.18 *Vertical view of finished deck centre section. Bed rolls in hammock netting.*

Fig 2.19 *Stern section of finished model showing whaler on davits, Captain's gig on stern davits.*

Fig 2.20 *The finished model on cradle stand. Name and details in mounted frame.*

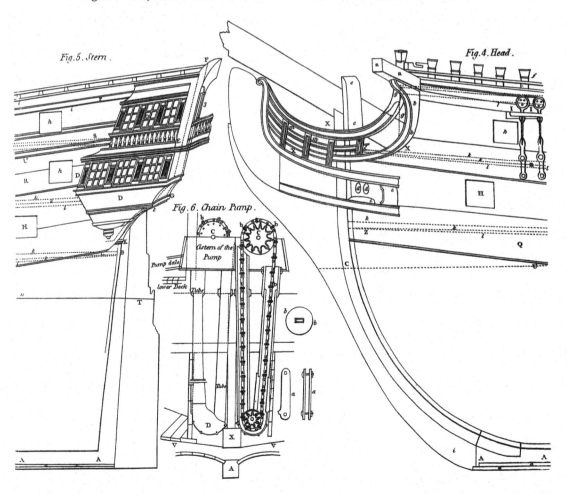

Fig 2.21 *An engraving from* The Treatise on Naval Affairs *in the* Royal Encyclopaedia *1791. The bow and stern of a 3rd Rater. Also shows a patent bilge pump.*

Fig 2.22 *As Fig. 2.21, but showing side view of a 1st Rater fully rigged.*

Main mast braces is usually the first cordage fitted, followed by main shrouds from deadeyes to tops.

The order of procedure from now on is all a matter of personal preference. I switch jobs around to avoid the boredom of some tasks. All yards and stuntsail booms are measured and made. The colour scheme follows roughly that of *HMS Victory* – buff yellow and black. A simple mahogany cradle-type mount was made and a few ship's details put in a small wooden frame fixed to the mount completed the job. (See **Figs 2.15** to **2.20** – the finished ship.)

Included in this chapter are reproductions of very old engravings. They are original pages from *The Treatise on Naval Affairs*. The engravings were for the *Royal Encyclopaedia* and published at various times, 1780, 1791 and 1816. They hang framed in my home as a source of inspiration for me to get on with another and better model and illustrate very well 1st, 2nd and 3rd Rater construction.

You can compare the drawings with photos of the famous 1st Rater *HMS Victory* at Portsmouth (see colour plates).

Although a rater system of divisions into which warships were grouped existed as early as the 1600s, in 1751 Admiral Lord Anson introduced the usually accepted version as follows:

- 1st Rater from 100 or 110 guns or more
- 2nd Rater from 84 to 100 guns
- 3rd Rater from 70 to 84 guns
- 4th Rater from 50 to 70 guns
- 5th Rater from 32 to 50 guns
- 6th Rater any number of guns up to 32 if commanded by a post-captain.

When commanded by a Commander these ships were rated as sloops of war.

Only the first three raters were considered sufficiently powerful to be in the direct line of battle in action between the main fleets. Fifth and sixth rate ships were generally known as frigates.

This rather long-winded explanation may help you recognise ship types of the navies in the 1700s and 1800s. So, if you find the making of small model cannons a bore, stick to the frigates, show all the gun ports closed and only show the upper deck guns!

Note: the plan I worked from is a Harold A. Underwood plan of a 3rd Rater (1813). There are seven sheets but I managed with just three. This is available at a number of outlets. *HMS Revenge*, launched in April 1805 was very similar to this plan. She took part at Trafalgar in October 1805.

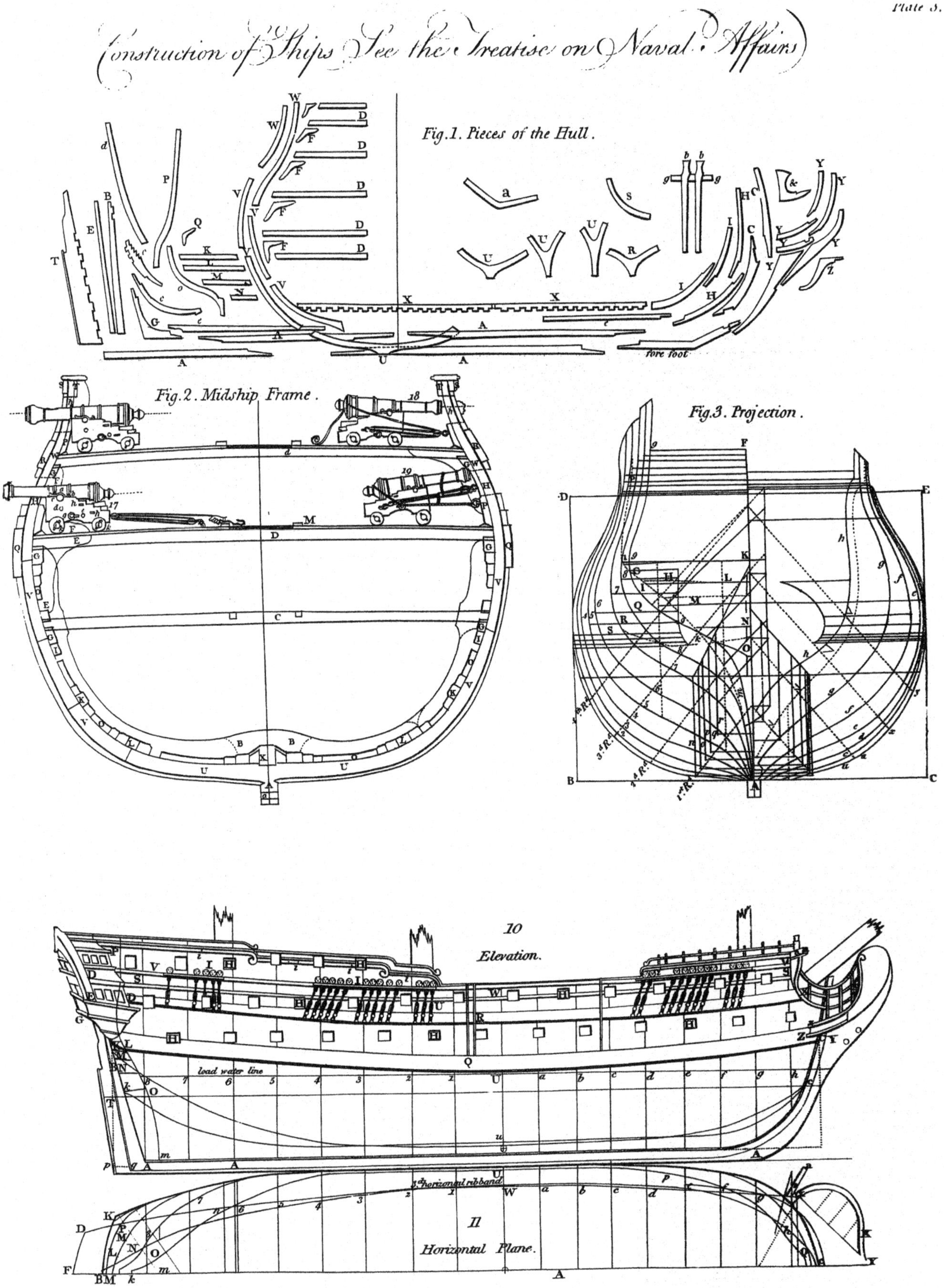

Plate 3.

Construction of Ships (See the Treatise on Naval Affairs)

Fig.1. *Pieces of the Hull.*

fore foot

Fig.2. *Midship Frame.*

Fig.3. *Projection.*

10

Elevation.

load water line

11

Horizontal Plane.

1st horizontal ribband

Fig 2.23 *An engraving from the Royal Encyclopaedia 1791 showing the construction details and timbers of a 3rd Rater.*

A cross-section model

If you have yet to make a model of one of the larger warships of the late 1700s and would like a project not so taxing, then try a cross-section model. It is rather like a dummy run before the big one.

Unfortunately I have no photographs of these interesting models, but the rough drawing (**Fig 2.26**) will give you an idea of the detail you can show.

It is usual to take about a six-inch section of the model to include the main mast. This would mean building only about four or five frames. The length will give you the opportunity to show a gun position on each deck and all the tackle, the main mast shrouds, chainplates and top etc. Furled sails will add to the charm of this kind of model. A nice stand, made of a piece of choice mahogany or oak, complete with polished brass title plate, finishes off the model.

After making one of these I guarantee you will be raring to have a go at the whole ship! When you have made it, you can show both models in the same display case.

Fig 2.24 The top deck entry port and steps of HMS Victory.

Fig 2.26 Drawing of a cross-section model showing a centre section with gun positions etc.

Fig 2.25 Close-up of Victory's chainplates.

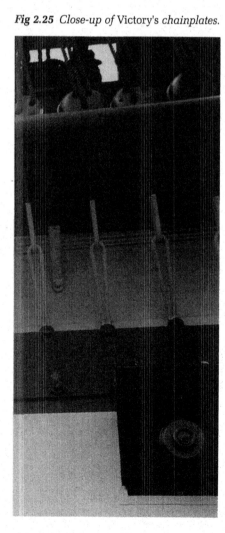

3 Another look at barges

My excuse for including barges once again in this latest book is that I am totally charmed by them. They are survivors, beasts of burden if you like, and we are still lucky enough to have quite a few knock-ing around to see and take notes from: St. Katherine Yacht Haven London, The Thames Sailing Barge Club, Malden, Essex and the Barge Museum, Crown Quay Lane, Sittingbourne, Kent, to mention

Fig 3.1 My latest model of Giralda *(Nexus Plans Service No. SY5). I doubled up the size from a 15in. hull to 30in. This allowed more space for good detailing as seen in the close-up shot. She was champion of the Thames races in most years between 1897 and 1904.*
Note: another good plan is that of the Kathleen *by Edgar J. March (Nexus Plans Service No. SY4).*

Fig 3.2 and 3.3 *This is my own version of an Ouse river barge of the last century. A friend asked me to make it as one of these had sunk in the mid 1800s in the river that flows past his old inn. Divers had noted its remains adjacent to the inn. Only a few photos were available for reference. Note no leeboard was deemed necessary on these craft.*

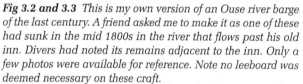

The gravel cargo in the forward hold is made from vermeculite mixed with a little Polycell. The main hold contains brick made from artists' clay, the logs and timber came from garden tree trimmings! There is also a small model wheelbarrow just to add to the authenticity.

Fig 3.4 *This is an oil painting by the author. It illustrates a view of the River Ouse at Lewes in Sussex at the turn of the century. The barges are of mixed variety.*

Fig 3.5 This is a picture taken at Lewes in Sussex of the Centaur *built at Harwich in 1895, seen here on the Harvey's Brewery quay in Lewes. She is very low in the water as if loaded but not very shipshape!*

just three places where you can indulge your interest.

To me, barges are a very English craft, ideally suited for our small islands with their numerous estuaries and waterways – not quite so many as in the barge's heyday unfortunately.

How barges evolved in the first place is interesting. The Dutch were certainly the leading early experts for vessels using leeboards. Again, having a watery country, the barge was an essential craft for the Dutch to develop.

Descriptions of the different types of barges are dealt with more fully in *Model Ships from Scratch*, so I will just list the types below for your reference:

- Thames coastal barge
- Thames river barge
- Stumpy barge
- Humber keel barge
- Norfolk wherry
- Dutch barge

To the expert, the pedigree of a barge is known immediately. The shape and size of the transom, bow shape and decorations will tell even the yard she was built in. See **Fig 3.13**.

The sailing barge is, no doubt, a development of the small early sailing trader like the hoy (see **Fig 3.10**) and this development carried on into the handsome craft of the turn of this century. Designs developed in other directions for cheap-to-build heavy load carriers. In America, broad beamed

Fig 3.6 A good photo of the Hetty *taken in the 1920s. Sharp-bowed, she reflects the more modern idea of a barge. No top mast on the main but a very high mizzen. She lies alongside the Phoenix Ironworks quay at Lewes in this photograph.*

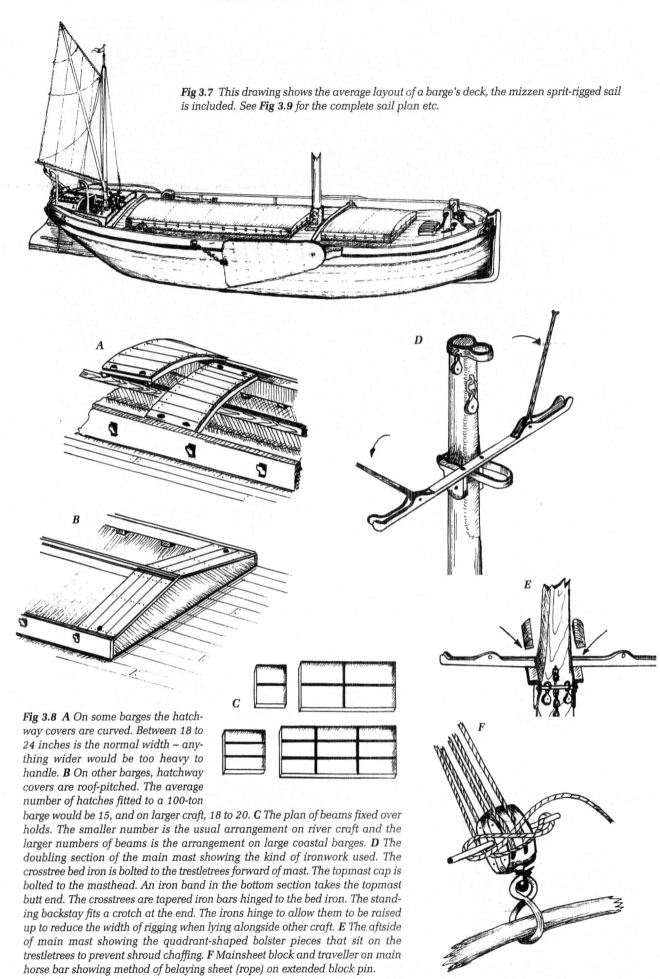

Fig 3.7 *This drawing shows the average layout of a barge's deck, the mizzen sprit-rigged sail is included. See* **Fig 3.9** *for the complete sail plan etc.*

A

B

C

D

E

F

Fig 3.8 **A** *On some barges the hatchway covers are curved. Between 18 to 24 inches is the normal width – anything wider would be too heavy to handle.* **B** *On other barges, hatchway covers are roof-pitched. The average number of hatches fitted to a 100-ton barge would be 15, and on larger craft, 18 to 20.* **C** *The plan of beams fixed over holds. The smaller number is the usual arrangement on river craft and the larger numbers of beams is the arrangement on large coastal barges.* **D** *The doubling section of the main mast showing the kind of ironwork used. The crosstree bed iron is bolted to the trestletrees forward of mast. The topmast cap is bolted to the masthead. An iron band in the bottom section takes the topmast butt end. The crosstrees are tapered iron bars hinged to the bed iron. The standing backstay fits a crotch at the end. The irons hinge to allow them to be raised up to reduce the width of rigging when lying alongside other craft.* **E** *The aftside of main mast showing the quadrant-shaped bolster pieces that sit on the trestletrees to prevent shroud chaffing.* **F** *Mainsheet block and traveller on main horse bar showing method of belaying sheet (rope) on extended block pin.*

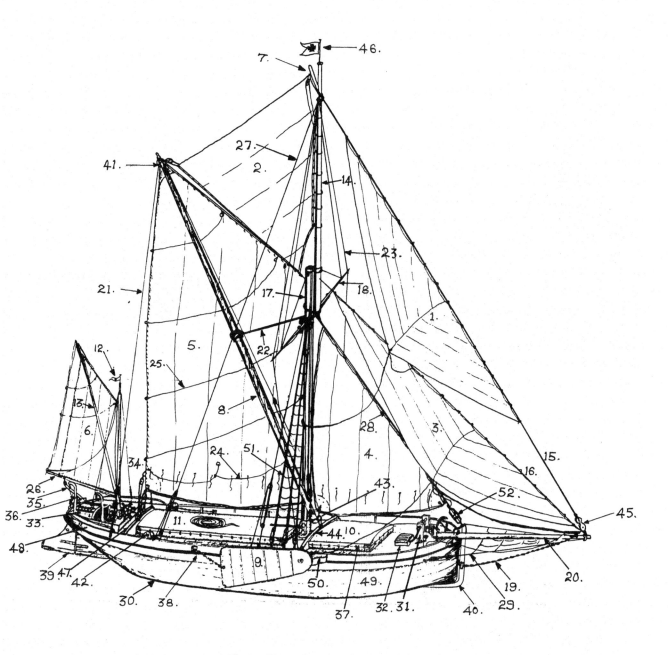

Fig 3.9 *Key to drawing of coastal barge*

1 Staysail-jib topsail
2 Topsail
3 Jib sail
4 Foresail
5 Mainsail
6 Mizzen/sail
7 Head stick
8 Sprit
9 Leeboard
10 Fore hatch
11 Main hatch
12 Mizzen mast
13 Mizzen sprit
14 Top mast
15 Top mast stay
16 Jibstay
17 Main mast
18 Crosstrees

19 Bobstay (chain)
20 Bowsprit
21 Vang or wang
22 Preventer stay
23 Standing backstay
24 Brailings
25 Main brail
26 Mizzen boom
27 Running backstays
28 Forestays
29 Bowsprit shrouds
30 Chine
31 Windlass
32 Fo'c'sle hatch
33 Cabin scuttle/hatch
34 Mizzen shrouds
35 Mizzen sheet

36 Davits
37 Fore hatch coamings
38 Pendant chain (½" chain)
39 Rudder
40 Stem
41 Sprit head
42 Leeboard crab/winch
43 Snotter gear on sprit butt
44 Fore horse
45 Stay sail pulley
46 Bob
47 Main horse
48 Quarter boards
49 Hull
50 Rigging chock
51 Starboard shroud
52 Stayfall tackle

Note *The base of the main mast is held in a lutchet, a kind of three-sided tabernacle. The aftside is missing so that the mast can be lowered. This box affords a fixing for two winches – one on either side.*

HOY

SAILING BARGE

Fig 3.10 An old engraving of sailing hoy and sprit-rigged barge.

Fig 3.11 The finished barge Giralda.

A

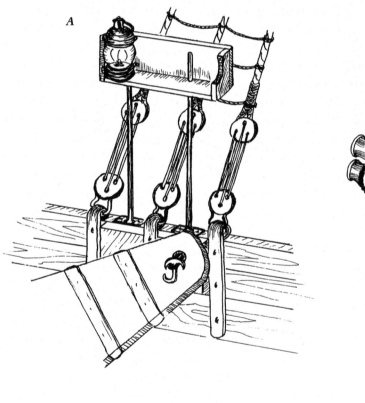

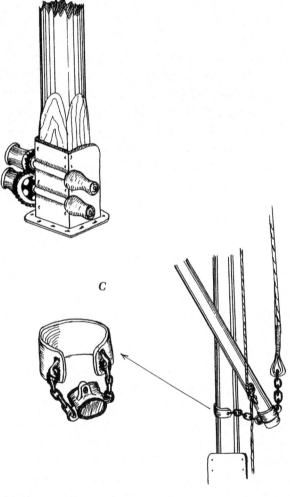

C

Fig 3.12 A *The deadeyes at the end of the shrouds are fixed directly to chainplates. Unlike a ship, the chainplate link does not go through a channel board but is bolted directly to the bulwark top. The patent light box can unhitch when necessary.* **B** *The mast case of a barge. In this case the metal trunk has two small winches on the face.* **C** *The snotter gear at the end of the mainsprit boom. It takes the weight and keeps the boom against the right side of the mast.*

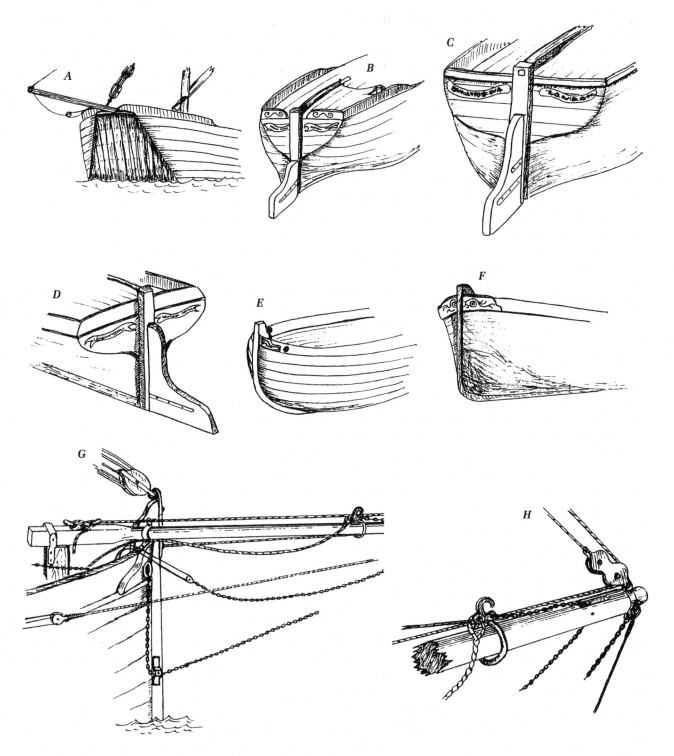

Fig 3.13 A *A swimhead and budget stern barge. Both punt-shaped ends of the vessel were similar. The rounded bow began to super-sede these in the 1850s. **B** An early transom type, small and narrow. **C** Later on, the transom was broadened taking on the shape of the type we can still see today. **D** A transom shape of about 1900. **E** A round bow, reminiscent of a Dutch barge. **F** A concave bow designed by Howard of Maldon. **G** The bow area of a barge showing the way the bowsprit is secured. The butt end rests on a block and is held by a strap. **H** Close-up of bowsprit on a barge. The ring traveller is pulled, in this case by a chain to the head of the bowsprit and back by rope.*

coastal traders did the job that our British barges carried out (see mention of this in Chapter 4).

The barge seems to belong to a different family of sailing boats. Its design and the gear found on these interesting vessels is different in many ways. The thickness of timbers and the obvious strength built into the hulls makes them one of the strongest and longest lasting boats you will find.

It was said that a barge was always practical before it was beautiful, and if it was beautiful, it was because it was right.

A barge is one of the best models for a beginner to

tackle. A solid block form will not be too difficult to shape and the hatch covers can be displayed covered, so the need for a hollow hull is not necessary.

In 1955 there were still 36 active sailing barges, 47 auxiliary sail barges and 80 motor barges. These were distributed between 38 different English owners. Some of the barges had building dates in the 1880s – this shows what tough vessels they were.

See Chapter 10, **Figs 10.8** and **10.12** for suggested methods of hull construction.

4 Gloucester schooners and other American craft

What is interesting about American working boats is that some are so different from our own British ones. To a modelmaker any increase in the choice of ships to model keeps the interest going.

The seas around our shores tend to dictate what our ships look like. This is well described in Eric McKee's book *Working Boats of Britain* (see Bibliography).

The American East coast from Boston to Washington was a wonderful breeding ground for many interesting working ships and smaller boats. There are some very interesting books on this subject, many reproductions from the originally first published versions, some of which are mentioned in the bibliography on page 125. The Nexus Plans Service has a few to choose from, others can be found in some of the books listed. These plans can be scaled up in various ways, and it is fun finding out the more involved detail of these ships.

I have listed below some types to look out for, a few of which I have featured in this chapter with photos of models I have made (indicated by a *).

- * Skipjack oystermen
- *Gloucester schooners
- *Dorys
- *American pilot boats
- Yawls
- Block Island boats
- *Pinkys
- Baltimore clippers
- New Haven sharpie
- Bermuda sloops
- Marblehead heel tapper
- American coastal traders

There are also many other schooner type coastal working ships to look out for.

The skipjack

In the Chesapeake Bay area of America a hard chine little working boat, said to have evolved from the New Haven sharpie, was developed in the 1870s. These 'diamond-bottom' craft were cheap to make and popular with amateur builders and professionals alike.

Farmers near the water could indulge in a spot of oyster catching in the season with homemade skipjacks.

The length of these craft varied from 28 to 60 feet. The larger boats used in the late 1890s were used mainly in the professional oyster business and all had drop centreboards.

This is a very easy little model to make. The plan comes from *American Sailing Craft* by Howard I. Chapelle. In my model the frames were made of ⅛in. ply and the skin was ¹⁄₃₂in. ply. The sides were in one piece allowing a very quick construction. See **Figs 4.1, 4.2, 4.3** and **4.4**.

In Chesapeake Bay, that boat-filled ocean inlet on the East coast of America, there are many islands, some marshy ones like Smiths Island, Tilgham and Deal Islands where, I am told, skipjacks can still be found. No new skipjacks have been built since about 1956 – a small ageing fleet still survived by virtue of a Maryland law designed to prevent over-harvesting of the oysters by motor vessels. Now that the famous bugeyes have gone (a two-masted fishing sailer with a similar hull to the skipjack) the skipjack is all that remains as a sailing oyster dredger on this famous stretch of water.

Gloucester schooners

The American fishing schooner can be traced back to around the 1780s. You can see the beginnings of this grand type of working ship in photos of models of a marblehead heel tapper in old books. Schooners in the early 1800s were more bluff-bowed until the launch of a new type in 1847. It took fishermen a long time to trust this sharper hull shape. Various changes to these new hulls were tried out but the fierce squalls of the fishing ground soon sorted out the best ideas.

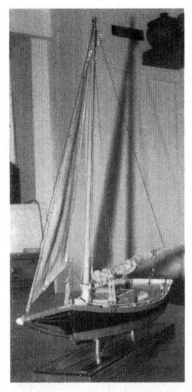

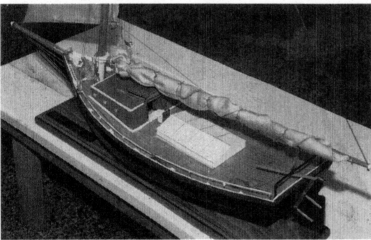

Figs 4.1, 4.2, 4.3, 4.4 *A finished model of an American skipjack. This one is a Chesapeake Bay oysterman, ¹⁄₁₆in. ply on ⅛in. frames.*

Captain Joseph William Collins came up with his ideal schooner in 1882. *Grampus* was built for the US Fish Commission. She had a shorter foremast than the main and wire rigging replaced the old hemp type.

She proved herself in 1886 sailing away from the fleet, close-hauled, with her fish to be first at the markets. Other designers copied the ideas and the race was on to even improve on the *Grampus*.

Various rigs were tried. The *Helen B. Thomas*, built in 1902, had no bowsprit, like the knockabout schooners of the 1890s. In 1906 Sir Thomas Lipton put up a permanent trophy for the annual Boston fishermen's race. This trophy increased the interest in building fast fishing schooners. *Rose Dorothea* (**Figs 4.5, 5A, 4.6A, 6B, 6C** and **6D**) won the race in 1907. Other famous schooners featured in these races, like the *Helen B. Thomas*, the *Metamora* (**Figs 6E** and **6F**), *Columbia* and the *Benjamin W. Laltham*.

Soon the Canadians were getting in on the act, wanting to prove their schooners. The Canadian bluenose raced against the *Elsie*, the US entry, in the International Fishermen's races in 1921.

Although I have concentrated on Gloucester fishing schooners, a mention should be made regarding the famous schooner yacht *America*. She was an out-and-out racing machine, a rich man's boat that raced in the Cowes event in England, to win the King's Cup for the New York Yacht Club in 1851. This race eventually became the America's Cup.

The *America* owes much to the cross-fertilisation of ideas caused by the development of the Gloucester schooner and the American pilot schooners.

Figs 4.5 and 4.5A *A solid carved hull in cedar of a Gloucester schooner* Rose Dorothea *1907.*

Figs 4.6A and 4.6B *Deck detail showing dory stowage and other fine detail.*

Figs 4.6C and 4.6D *The finished model of Gloucester schooner* Rose Dorothea *1907.*

Figs 4.6E and 4.6F *The finished model of the Gloucester schooner* Metamora.

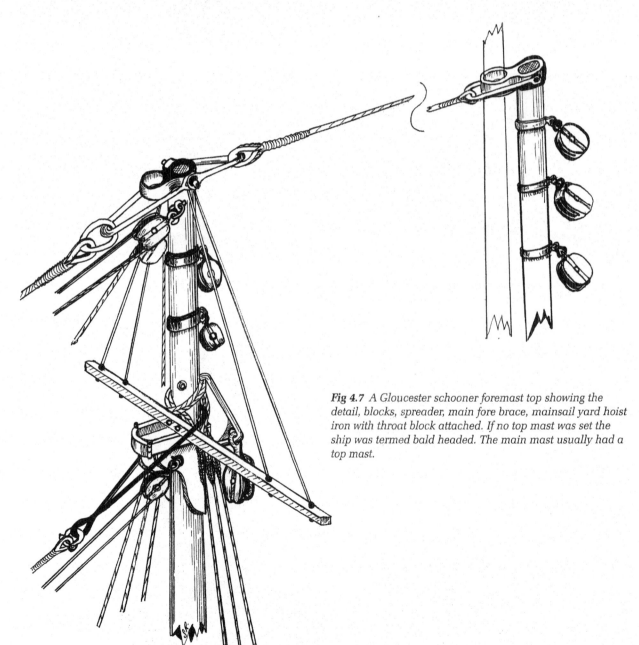

Fig 4.7 *A Gloucester schooner foremast top showing the detail, blocks, spreader, main fore brace, mainsail yard hoist iron with throat block attached. If no top mast was set the ship was termed bald headed. The main mast usually had a top mast.*

Many of these craft were designed by the famous George Steers, who also designed the *America*.

The Nexus Plans Service have a Grand Bank schooner Plan No. MM 962. There is also a schooner Plan No. MM 405. This is not strictly a Grand Banker, but a handsome craft of this type. See **Fig. 4.14**. Both models featured as photos, the *Rose Dorothea* and the *Metamora* were carved from solid cedar wood, a separate piece was made for the keel and joined to the hull after carving.

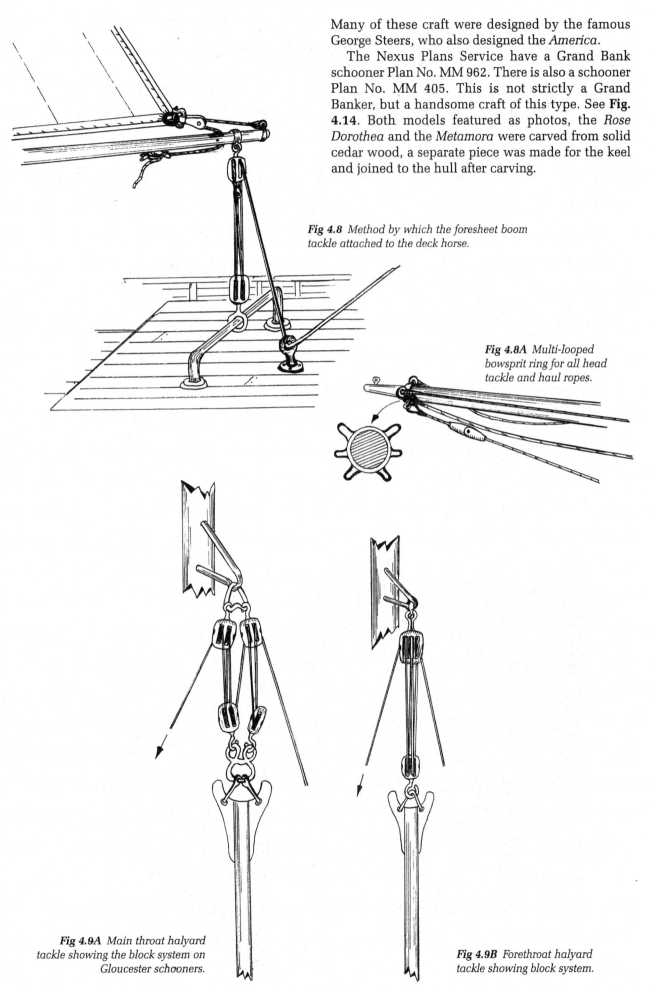

Fig 4.8 *Method by which the foresheet boom tackle attached to the deck horse.*

Fig 4.8A *Multi-looped bowsprit ring for all head tackle and haul ropes.*

Fig 4.9A *Main throat halyard tackle showing the block system on Gloucester schooners.*

Fig 4.9B *Forethroat halyard tackle showing block system.*

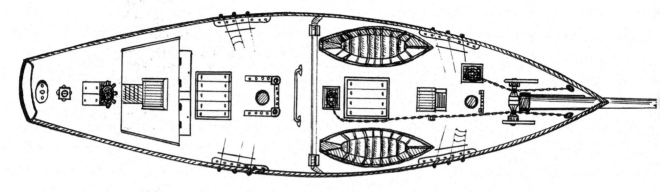

Fig 4.10 *General deck layout of a Gloucester schooner at the turn of the century.*

Fig 4.11 *Dory men fishing away from the mother vessel and a line plan of a standard dory.*

Fig 4.12 *A real dory under construction showing the simple method of building. The same dory completed with the sails fitted.*

Fig 4.13 *A Bude dory photographed in Cornwall in 1985.*

Fig 4.14 *A model of the* George Steer, *an American pilot boat.*

Dorys

This famous type of ships' boat should really be included in Chapter 6 on ships' boats, but I am giving it a separate mention here.

Writing in *Yachting Monthly* magazine, somebody suggested that if you were asked to design a cheap small ships' boat, measuring between 17ft and 19ft long, that could easily carry half a ton of wet fish, light enough to be launched by hand and reclaimed by the mother ship at a rate of perhaps twenty to thirty times in twenty minutes and then put back in the water again, you would be hard put to come up with something good. It would have to be strong enough to be thumped and bumped alongside the ship or beached through surf when necessary. Well, the traditional dory is such a craft. Some call it a Portuguese dory where its origins may well lie. The Nexus Plans Service have a plan No. MM 563 for a 1/10 scale model.

Some years ago I made a small model, but unfortunately I have no photographs. I can, however, show you a picture of a real dory I made after the model was finished and I can certainly confirm all that has been said about these wonderful little working ships' boats. See **Figs 4.11, 4.12** and **4.13**.

On the Grand Bank schooners, the dorys were stacked inside one another, each side amidships – thwart seats could be removed to aid this. Various writers have claimed different numbers of the fishing dorys stacked on the mother ship, six a side or as many as twelve a side, depending on the schooner's size. I made my model schooners with four a side. After making eight of these I gave up. See **Fig 4.6**.

American pilot boats

This type of craft was fast and very seaworthy. Designs varied, depending on the working location. New York, Boston and ports in Virginia all made these pilot schooners in the 1850s and 1860s.

Howard I. Chapelle describes these craft in *American Sailing Craft* far better than I can, but there are many plans in the book to excite the modelmaker. The *George Steer*, a Sandy Hook pilot schooner No. 6 was considered to be one of the most elegant and my plank-on-frame model tries to show this – see **Fig 4.14**.

Very few of these of these ships died of old age, but many floundered doing their duty in the difficult East coast waters of America. The *George Steer*

Fig 4.15 *Joshua Slocum's yawl* Spray.

was driven ashore on the Jersey coats near Barnegat in a bad north-easter on 12th February 1865 with the loss of all five crew.

Sloop into a yawl

A charming little ship called *Spray* is included for those interested in simple uncomplicated modelling. If you have a lust for nautical stories, Captain Joshua Slocum's *Sailing Alone Around the World* should grab the imagination of any modelmaker. I have included some line drawings that may be of help in modelling her. See **Figs 4.15** and **4.16**.

The story of *Spray* is worth a brief mention because it is unique. In 1892, Captain Slocum was considering his future and wondering where his next command would come from when he met an old acquaintance, Captain Eben Pierce, in Boston. Captain Pierce made him an offer that was to change Captain Slocum's life and give history a wonderful story – "Come to Fairhaven and I'll give you an old ship".

The hulk, an old sloop, had sat in a field for seven years some way from immediate saltwater. The locals said it had first served as a local oysterman and was probably built a little under a hundred years earlier. Captain Slocum decided to rebuild her completely and after fourteen months, a lot of hard toil and the cost of $553.62 she was launched in 1894.

A robust little craft, she measured 36ft 19in. in length and 14ft 11in. in the beam, of carvel planked construction measuring 1½in. thick of Georgia pine. She sailed around the world, leaving Boston in April 1895 and returning there in July 1898. During the trip Captain Slocum changed the rig from sloop to yawl by reducing the mainsail area and adding a jigger mast with mizzen lug sail – this helped when allowing the *Spray* to sail herself with a lashed wheel.

This story was first published in America in 1900, and later by Rupert Hart-Davis in the UK in 1948.

To make a model of *Spray* should not be too difficult. Carvel planking on twelve frames should make a nice hull. The profile drawings indicate the sail plan as sloop or yawl (see **Fig 4.16**) and the other drawing indicates the deck layout. The Nexus Plans Service can supply its version of *Spray*, No.V 113. This is a sailing model by Vic Smeed with a 30in. long hull.

Note: it is interesting to see that *Spray* is mentioned in *The Oxford Companion to Ships and the Sea* as one of the hull shapes listed in the evolution of the yacht hull.

The list includes:

- Revenue cutter 1781
- *America* 94ft 1851
- *Jullanar* 110ft 1875
- *Gloriana* 70ft 1891
- *Spray* 37ft 1894

I would add to this Baltimore clippers and Gloucester schooners.

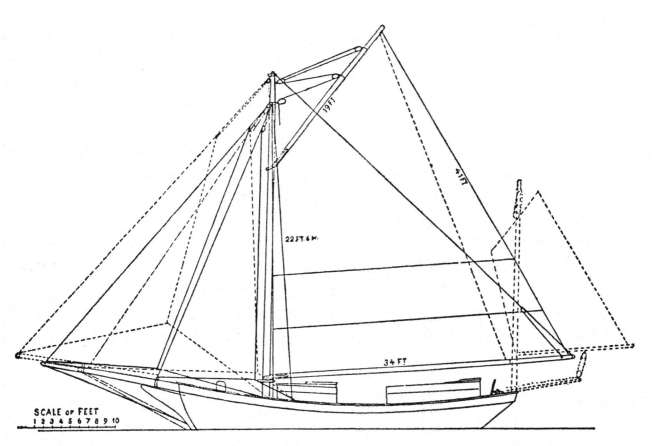

Fig 4.16 The yawl Spray.

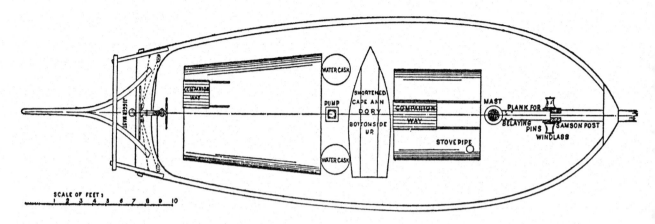

Fig 4.16A *Plan of* Spray.

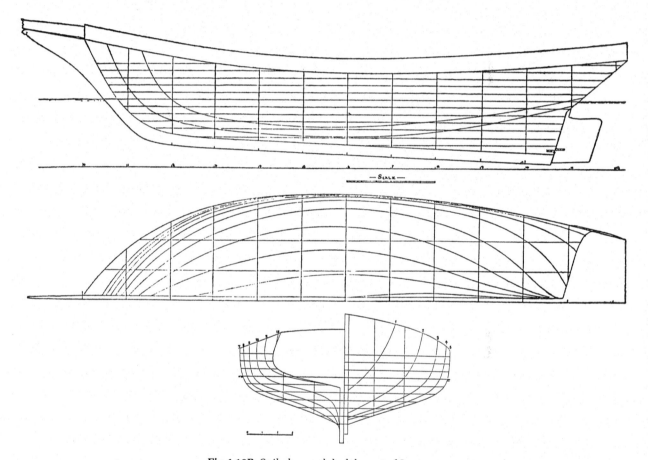

Fig 4.16B *Sail plan and deck layout of* Spray.

Pinkys

Pink or pinkys is a word used to describe certain types of boats from as long ago as the 15th and 16th centuries.

The word 'pink' described a square-rigged ship with a narrow overhanging stern, often used for carrying masts. It also described small ships with narrow sterns. A pinky is one of the oldest types of New England fishing and trading vessels with a stern, which is similar to the bows, carried well out beyond the rudder like a counter stern, resembling a North Sea Danish pink of the early 18th century from which the name originates. Schooner-rigged, with or without a forestay sail or jib, these pink-sterned boats were used for many different purposes.

One of the main centres where they were built was in the parish of Chebacco (now the town of Essex, Massachusetts) and in the town of Ipswich before the Revolution where they were used for fishing the nearby banks. After the Revolution, the

Fig 4.17 American pinky, a schooner-rigged model of the Eagle 1820.

larger pinkys turned to privateering. Some were very big at around thirty tons, but many of the smaller ones of five to six tons were home-built. The deck plans of these craft varied considerably depending on the job for which they were used.

The model illustrated is a fishing boat – the pinky *Eagle* of 1820. The plans are taken from the splendid book by Charles G. Davis *American Sailing Ships, Their Plans and History*. See **Fig 4.17**.

The American coastal trader

This type of craft can give you a lot of pleasure to make as a model. Schooner-rigged with two and sometimes three masts, these craft had various local names depending on the different cargoes they carried. For instance, boxboards were lumber carriers, stone droghers carried various granites and other rocks. There were packets and bay coasters that plied their trade well into the 1930s, supplying remote villages and towns of Eastern Maine and carrying every conceivable item.

Other names are mentioned in the very interesting book by John F. Leavitt called *Wake of the Coasters* (see Bibliography). Sailing scows and the New Brunswick wood schooners called locally 'Johnny wood bo'ts' to mention two.

You may find it difficult to locate plans of these turn-of-the-century vessels but there are plans of English trading schooners available. The Nexus Plans Service have available an English sailing coaster No. MM 1324 *Julia May*. This is a bread-and-butter section hull with a length of 30in. It is a two-masted sailer but makes a splendid static model.

5 *Alabama III* – a complete picture story of the model construction

I make no apology for featuring *Alabama* once again in this new collection of model ships. I have called it No. III as two smaller models, I and II were illustrated in my first book, *Model Ships from Scratch*.

I have included it here because makers will find it much easier to work on the detail if they enlarge any ⅛ scale plan to ³⁄₁₆ scale, like this new model described.

Marine archaeologists have now located the wreck of the original ship off Cherbourg, so keep your eyes skinned for any further press mention. Below is a brief history of this interesting vessel for those who may not be acquainted with the *CSS Alabama*.

British-built – the cream of the Confederate Navy

At the beginning of the American Civil War, the Southern states virtually had to build a navy from scratch. They looked to Europe, and to Great Britain in particular, for new and modern ships that could be used to raid and harass Northern states' shipping as their own ports and shipbuilding areas were suffering from Lincoln's blockade.

President Jefferson Davis and his cabinet decided to send marine agent experts to Great Britain and Europe to buy and organise the arming of these vessels. This was a difficult project in view of British neutrality prohibiting ships from being armed for war in England. However, this little problem was soon overcome using varied and devious methods, finally costing all those involved on this side of the Atlantic $15,500,500 in gold reparations, known as the 'Alabama Claim' after the war had finished.

The most successful of these Confederate naval agents was James D. Bulloch who landed in Liverpool on 4th June 1861. The Laird shipyards at Birkenhead featured in his search for new vessels, as did other yards in this country. The *Florida* was the first ship to be purchased, quickly followed by

the famous *Alabama*. She slipped away secretly on 29th July 1862, just avoiding being impounded by the British authorities. She sailed down to the Azores to be armed and victualled. For twenty-two months the *Alabama* brought havoc to the Northern states' commercial and naval shipping.

Of the twelve famous major ships of the Confederate Navy, six were either built or bought in this country, namely *Florida*, *Alabama*, *Shenandoah*, *Georgia*, *Talahassee* and the *Chickamauga* – the first three being the results of James Bulloch's efforts.

The *Alabama* captured, destroyed or ransomed some sixty-four prizes during her twenty-two months of sailing. She herself was sunk in the famous battle with the *Kearsarge*, a Union gunboat, on the morning of 19th July 1864, three miles off Cherbourg.

In 1984 a French Navy sonar sweep found the original wreck. At the time these waters were considered international but they are now French waters and thus this wreck has been claimed by the French, setting off a real squall between French, British and American marine archaeologists about what belongs to whom! Even in death *Alabama* remains a controversial ship.

Making the model

Some of the ships named here are a real challenge to construct from scratch. I chose the *Alabama* simply because this ship seems to have attracted more records, plans and details than others of the period.

The plans of the CSS Alabama
My main plan comes from the Nexus Plans Service No. MM1027. This gives a very good basis to work from. I enlarged it by half as much again to enable as much detail as possible to be included. Another valuable source of information was *CSS Alabama – Builder, Captain and Plans* by Charles Grayson Summersell (1985, University of Alabama Press).

An original set of Lairds plans can be found in a pouch at the back of this book. Early contemporary photography can sometimes be found in library books on these Confederate ships. Although *Alabama* was an all-wooden ship, similar types were being built as ironclads or composites of wood and steel (see **Fig 5.25**). It was a time of great change in ship construction which is what makes them so interesting.

The hull

The hull was built on ⅛in. ply frames and planked in 2mm thick lime (see **Figs 5.1** to **5.3**). Some of these planks were 6mm wide, others 4mm wide. Stem to stern beams were made of plain pine. The deck was first covered with a layer of ⅟₃₂in. thick ply before covering with the lime planks (4mm wide type). This gave a firm deck base. All plank fixings were glued with PVA and nailed using 7mm brass pin nails. I used a small toffee hammer and tweezers for these little devils!

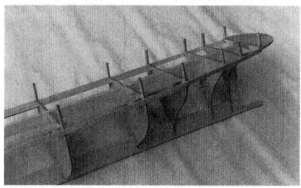

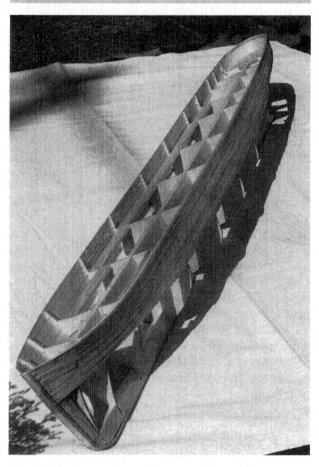

Fig 5.3 The hull with some planks attached.

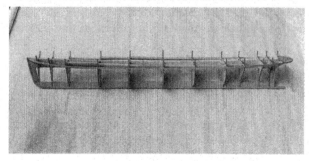

Fig 5.1 and 5.2 The hull frame before planking.

Polyfilla was then applied over the whole exterior of the planked hull and sanded down well after thoroughly drying this coating (see **Figs 5.4** and **5.5**).

As you can see from the photos, the bulkhead frames include the timberheads that stick up above the deck line. The exterior plank cladding comes to the top of these timberheads, as does the interior

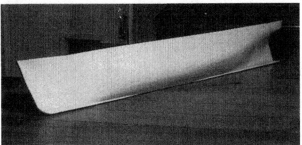

Fig 5.4 and 5.5 Planking completed with Polyfilla *coating applied and rubbed down.*

bulwark cladding (see **Figs 5.3** and **5.6**). The curve of the stern bulwark is always a problem. Steaming or wetting the small lime planks I decided was not

Fig 5.6 Interior bulwark planking applied.

the method to use. Thick card was used instead, in two laminations, taking careful templates first. The small windows under the stern were also made of card, carefully pierced with a scalpel, painted white and glued onto an already painted black stern area, see **Fig 5.15**.

As the model has such a strong shroud and rigging arrangement I simply drilled the deck for masts going ½in. into a fairly robust centre deck beam. Later, when glued in place, the masts held up well whilst rigging was completed.

Gun ports and other piercings

If you have managed to get all your frames exactly placed within the hull, the gun ports should not be a problem. Using a fine jewellery saw, the ports were cut down from top of the gunwale to deck level, removed and numbered carefully. When the crew used the two big gauge guns (see list of armaments at end), the whole side was removed. The six 32lb guns had side-hinged double-door ports. As the ports would be closed on this model all the pieces already removed were cleaned up and glued back in place after adjusting their thickness (see **Figs 5.7** and **5.8**). This gives a good impression of a real gun port that is closed even if it does take a little more time. Belaying pin rails were then attached to the inside of the bulwarks.

When you are satisfied that hull and sides are all nice and clean, paint the inside of the bulwarks and give the hull a coat of paint. At this stage I coated the decks with two coats of matt varnish. Establish the correct waterline from the plans (by this time you should be working on some sort of temporary stand). Using the usual method of a level table,

Fig 5.7 and 5.8 Deck planks in place. Gun ports fitted and painted.

position the hull, draw a pencil line or scribe a line using a block of wood of the correct height right around the hull carefully. See Chapter 10, **Fig 10.12**.

Chainplates and shroud fixings

I find it easier to fix the chainplates onto a finished painted hull. You can always touch this up if any marks are made. Always drill with a small hand chuck the holes for the nails fixing the chainplates to the hull, having carefully angled all these to the mast top fixing points as per the plan. These small holes are always drilled under-size for the nails. I used the toffee hammer to punch these through the drilled chainplates onto the hull.

I decided to use the new type of connections, bottle screws, for attaching the shrouds to the chainplates. Deadeyes were becoming redundant due to the new wire cables used on standing rigging for these new warships. Jewellery screw connectors for necklaces were a convincing shape (see **Fig 5.18**).

Deck details

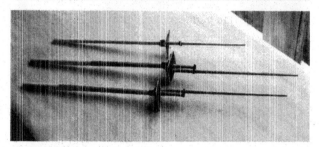

Fig 5.12 and 5.13 Masts pre-constructed ready for mounting.

Most of this can be completed now. Hatch covers, fife rails, ships' wheel and binnacle etc. (see **Figs 5.18** and **5.19**). Ships' boats, of which there are five, were all carved in balsa wood. Quarter decks and seats were later glued in using ⅟₃₂in. ply sheet (see **Fig 5.11**). Davits were made from brass brazing rods. Masts were pre-made (see **Figs 5.12** and **5.13**). These were erected on the hull after colouring etc.

I didn't buy much – a double ship's wheel, air vent in brass, two anchors, brass nails and all the lime planking. *Maritime Models of Greenwich* were most helpful and sent all these by return of post after ordering by phone. Cordage was dyed where appropriate and made up by spin twisting. Blocks

Fig 5.9 and 5.10 Chainplates and deck furniture completed ready for masting. Steering wheel and binnacle fitted.

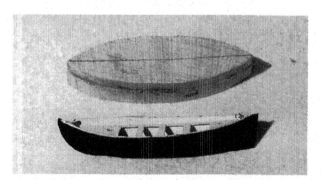

Fig 5.11 One of the ship's boats completed, hand-carved from balsa wood.

Fig 5.14 Main mast yard and top showing studding sail booms.

were made by hand.

List of armaments

The *Alabama* had eight guns – six 32-pounder guns of 55cwt each, a 7in. rifled pivot gun 100-pounder, and an 8in. solid shot 68-pounder smooth bore, this gun was also provided with shell as well as shot. Two big arms chests at the stern held hand guns and rifles. All these were hand-made using wood dowel and metal tubes etc. Painted matt black they looked convincing. See general deck photos (**Figs 5.16** and **5.18**). The 7in. rifled 100-pounder Blakeley pivot gun has now been raised from the wreck and is being overhauled in France. A live primed shell was found in the breech which was considered still to be lethal after 130 years under the sea!

The plinth

This was made from a slab of mahogany that used to be a pub bar top at my local until it was redecorated. The model was mounted on two stout brass rods. A brass 'U' piece supported the centre to strengthen and prevent any tendency for the hull to wobble. The case was a very professional job by a local craftsman. See **Fig 5.28**.

Fig 5.15 Stern showing gingerbreading, carved in semi-dry Polyfilla *and gilded.*

Fig 5.16 Deck view of bow section with anchor chains and 32-pounder cannons in bow chaser position.

Fig 5.17 Port side ship's boats with hammocks stowed in gunwhale top. These were made of Rizla *cigarette paper filters bent double.*

Fig 5.18 Deck, mid hull section.

Fig 5.19 Stern deck and ship's wheel detail.

Fig 5.20 and 5.21 Side view on temporary support.

Fig 5.22 *Stern view, showing brass frame holding ship's details.*

Fig 5.23 *A model shipwright's model made at Bassett Lowke. A beautiful model and something to aim for!*

Fig 5.24 *An old print of the sinking of* Alabama *by the Kearsarge 19th July 1864.*

Fig 5.25 *This interesting modern photo of* HMS Warrior, *an early ironclad, sailing neck and neck with* HMS Arrow *after her facelift in Hartlepool on her way to Portsmouth, where you can now see her. She has similar lines to* Alabama *and well illustrates the progress of this type of warship. She was originally launched in 1860. There is a 5-sheet plan available for* Warrior *by David Metcalf & William Mowll, Nexus Plans Service No. MM1397 (C.O.I. picture).*

Fig 5.26 *A deck view looking forward on* Warrior *at Portsmouth.*

Fig 5.27 *A large shell firing gun in bow area of* Warrior. *This was an early breech loader (Armstrong, rifled breech loader 100lb).*

Fig 5.28 Alabama – *the finished model, cased.*

6 Ships' boats and nautical dioramas

Ships' boats

When making model ships one is liable to forget the need to show convincing ship seaboats and other oar-propelled craft which were so important to the average commercial craft or warship. Many plans rather ignore this side of detailing, showing only perhaps an outline and position indicators. I don't mind admitting that I find them difficult to make, but I would much rather have homemade ones than the plastic, bought types. Having said that, it is sometimes useful to buy one of these plastic boats and use it as a reference for your own modelmaking in wood.

Below I have tried to cast some light on this subject and list some of the types you are likely to come across in modelling old ships.

There is a certain basic beauty in the lines of these small boats. There must be something about their good lines of design and seaworthiness to have stood the test of time, for they changed very little over the years. These boats, especially the larger ones, were extremely versatile, being used for towing the mother ship caught in the doldrums, mounting small calibre cannons on cutting out expeditions and making epic journeys over thousands of miles like Captain Bligh of *Mutiny on the Bounty* fame.

They sported many different sailing rigs when conditions were suitable as sails gave the crew a rest from rowing over longer distances.

A brief description of each type of boat is listed below which may help you understand this particular ship's detail when making the big one!

Launch

The launch was usually the largest ship's boat (as it is today). There were usually two of these, the smaller known as the Captain's barge, the larger one known as the longboat in the 18th and 19th centuries. Carvel-built with mast and sails for short sea expeditions was usual. Pulling twelve or fourteen oars, double-banked, they could also accommodate a ship's cannon in the bows.

Its principal use to the ship was the transporting of heavy stores, shore-to-ship and the carting of water casks ashore for fresh water on long sea journeys. As the principal ship's boat it also served as the main lifeboat. Dry provisions and a water cask were permanently stored on board.

The developed version of the launch became the major warship's boat in the 19th and 20th centuries. Its size varied widely between 26 and 32ft long.

Cutters

A clinker-built ship's boat measuring 24–32ft long, pulling eight to fourteen oars depending on size. It can be rigged with two masts and lug sails. This is a much faster boat than the launch. To save space on old warships they were stowed inside the launches – there were usually two.

Fig 6.1 A rather splendid boat at the Navy Museum on the hard at Portsmouth adjacent to HMS Victory and HMS Warrior. *It is a King Charles II state barge – a shallow draft boat known as a shallop.*

49

Fig 6.2 *A 1930s whaler turned into a motor sailer. The more modern whalers had a drop keel – this gave the hull excellent sailing characteristics. The shape is very similar to the old ones as you can see.*

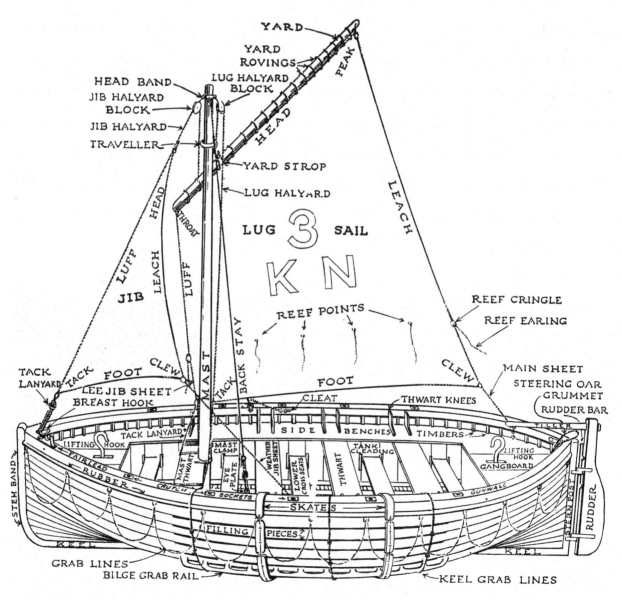

Fig 6.3 *An old print of a standard pre~war lifeboat. The drawing is rather squat but it names all the parts rather well.*

Fig 6.4 *A pre-war ship's lifeboat converted into a small fishing boat. These were the kind of boats seen on the davits of liners before and during the war. Nowadays they are less graceful and made of metal in many cases.*

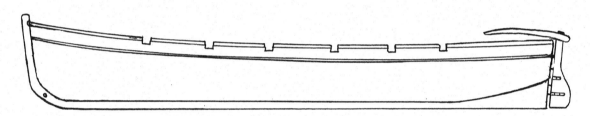

Fig 6.5 *Profile drawing of launch.*

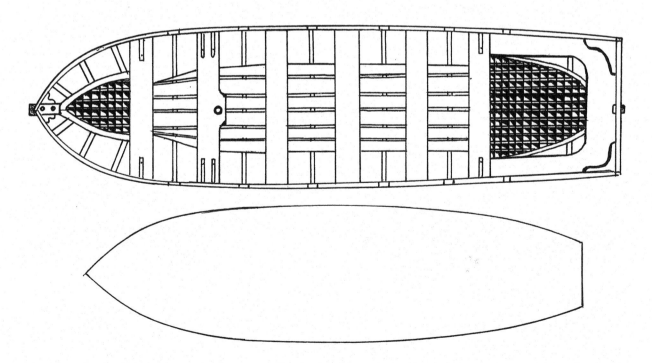

Fig 6.6 *Plan of launch showing seats etc. Plan outline only of cutter. These are stowed inside the launches.*

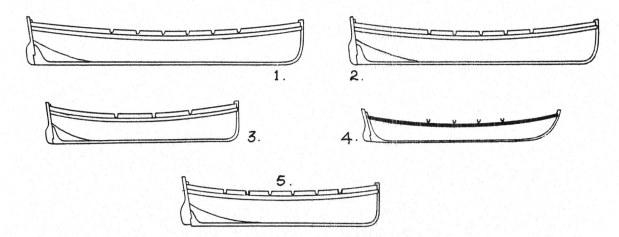

Fig 6.7 *1 Launch profile. 2 Cutter profile. 3 Yawl profile. 4 Whaler profile. 5 Pinnace profile.*

Pinnace

On average the pinnace was slightly smaller than the above boats described. In Nelson's time this type was hung on davits for immediate launching. Eighteen feet long was a useful size. Originally it was used with eight oars but later increased in length to use sixteen oars. One of its uses was carrying messages between ships whilst in convoy. The larger pinnace could step a mast when required and set a sloop rig.

Whaler

This boat was sharp both ends and again hung on davits. The design was taken from the original whaling boat tender with an average size around 18ft pulling oars. Yawl-rigged with triangular jib and mizzen with gunter mainsail.

The first whaler was on the port side rear davit, with the second whaler on rater ships hung on stern davits which was sometimes called the Captain's gig.

Yawl

A clinker-built, robust ship's boat pulling six oars. Yawl was a term used in the 19th century and describes the position of masts rather than a particular rig of sails. Any boat with main mast, cutter rigged and a mizzen stepped well back or abaft the rudder was termed yawl.

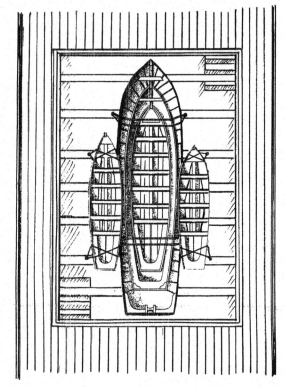

Fig 6.9 *Stowage of ship's boats on a capital warship in the 1800s.*

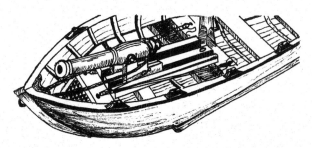

Fig 6.8 *An impression of a light cannon mounted in the prow on recoil sliders and braced. Pinnaces and launches were sometimes used in this fashion.*

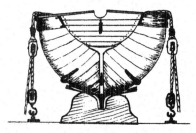

Fig 6.9A *One of the methods of stowage for a ship's boat on deck. Note: The average number of ship's boats carried by a 3rd Rater was seven. No.1 and No.2 launches, No.1 and No.2 cutters, stowed inside launches, 1 pinnace and 1 whaler hung in davits – port and starboard. 1 whaler on stern davits (Captain's gig).*

Fig 6.10A A Gloucester schooner in harbour alongside fish warehouses etc. (an imaginary tableaux).

Fig 6.10B A terrarium bottle containing a model. These come in various sizes so choose one with the largest neck opening.

The above descriptions of the five main types of ships' boats are those found on period warships. Small types were certainly used like dinghies, skiffs and other small pulling boats. Large commercial sailers and square-rigged vessels copied the naval boats in most cases.

I know of some modelmakers who make wonderfully accurate models of these small boats. There is a good *Panart* plan from a kit for an armed pinnace c.1803 – this is fully rigged with cannon in the prow and a small bore gun mounted on the gunnel.

Some of these small models command high prices. At Christies maritime sale they fetch hundreds of pounds for really superior models and they are beautiful examples of the craft of modelling.

Nautical dioramas and tableaux

These interesting models can sometimes be seen in museums. They come in all sizes but the more manageable sizes come cased, depicting harbour scenes. Waterline models alongside moorings, adjacent to warehouses and workshops, make it interesting. Sometimes full hull models on the hard, being built, give the scene reality.

Obviously the imagination can take over a project like this. If they are well constructed with an interesting layout, much pleasure can be obtained making them. They don't have to be large – it is amazing what you can put on a two foot by eighteen inch board. See **Fig 6.10A**.

If this seems daunting, and you have tried a ship in a bottle, then try a small fishing harbour in a large glass terrarium bottle. You can buy these in gardening shops and centres. They have larger mouths than the average carboy and are far easier to work with than bottling a ship model. Although the bottles are meant to contain a planted garden of growing plants they make excellent containers for our models.

The bottle necks are anything from two inches to five inches across, so a single ship model of reasonable proportions placed on a putty sea is not out of the question, and it will save you making a case! See **Fig 6.10B**.

For a model in a glass terrarium use the same technique as you would for a ship in a bottle (see Chapter 1).

HMS Victory *at her permanent moorings in Portsmouth.*

The finished model of the Gloucester schooner Metamora.

Detailed view of CSS Alabama, *finished model.*

Finished model of PS Britannia.

A life-size reproduction of Drake's Golden Hind *at Brighton, 1996.*

A Lowestoft drifter trawler.

A recently completed model of the brig-sloop HMS Grasshopper, *later named* Irene *after capture by the Dutch in 1811. Launched at Hythe in 1806.*

7 Steamers and paddle steamers

If you want to indulge in a little pre-war nostalgia look no further than the paddle steamer. Some readers will certainly remember seeing these ships bulging with holidaymakers as they plodded from port to port. There are one or two still about – the *Waverley* was still on active service last year. She looks very like the *Britannia* (see my model, **Figs 7.1** and **7.2**)

Excursion paddle steamers make interesting models and there are plenty of plans about. Other countries have their own interesting steamers, the Mississippi sternwheeler and the steamers of the Nile being good examples.

Below I have listed some plans from the Nexus Plans Service of old paddle steamers:

Fig 7.1 Finished model of PS Britannia, *43in. long. Plan No. MM1336.*

Fig 7.2 PS Britannia. *Close-up of bridge, funnels and paddle box.*

Paddle steamers

- MM 1375 *Bournemouth Queen* This is large – 54in. long – you could reduce the plans though.
- MM 1401 *Hiawatha*, American coastal paddle boat.
- MM 1153 *PS Bilsdale* 1900, 35in. long.
- MM 1242 *Marchioness of Larne* A Clyde PS 44in. long.
- MM 1336 *Britannia* 43in. long. (See **Fig 7.1**)
- MM 1374 *Iona* Thames paddle tug 41in. long.

There are many other plans for old steamers and tugs if you are looking for a change from square riggers.

Fig 7.3 The steam yacht Medea, *finished and cased. A brass photo frame contains the ship's history.*

The River Dart in Devon had many interesting steam-driven craft. The fleet list of the River Dart Steamboat Company was long and varied, starting with the iron paddler *Eclair* 1865, a two-funnelled craft plying the route from Dartmouth to Guernsey and the last ship, the *Cardiff Castle* 1964.

My little model of the *PS Compton Castle* was built using the slab-side form of hull construction – see **Figs 7.4**, **7.5** and **7.6** and Chapter 10. She joined their fleet in 1914. She was sold for scrap in 1962 but bought back in 1963 and turned into a cafe and museum at Kingsbridge, Devon.

The gentleman's steam yacht is another type of interesting vessel. The *Medea* 1904 was featured in my last book as a good example of this type. Built in Glasgow, she is now still afloat at the San Diego Museum – see **Fig 7.3**. The plans were reproduced very small in *Model Shipwright* magazine March 1987, Number 59.

The detail is more simple on this type of model. I find the hull shapes easier to make and the paddle boxes are certainly an interesting feature. With a static model you really only need to show half a paddle, it is up to you. See **Fig 7.7**. This plan of the *PS Compton Castle* comes from a little eight-page booklet by Bryan Moseley, first published in 1965 which tells the story about River Dart shipping.

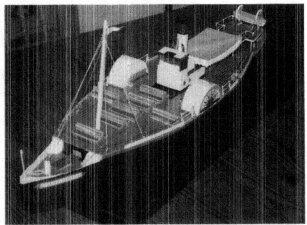

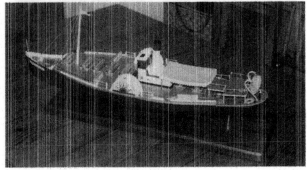

Fig 7.4 to 7.6 The PS Compton Castle *1914, one of the fleet of the River Dart Steamboat Co., now a permanent museum at Kingsbridge, Devon.*

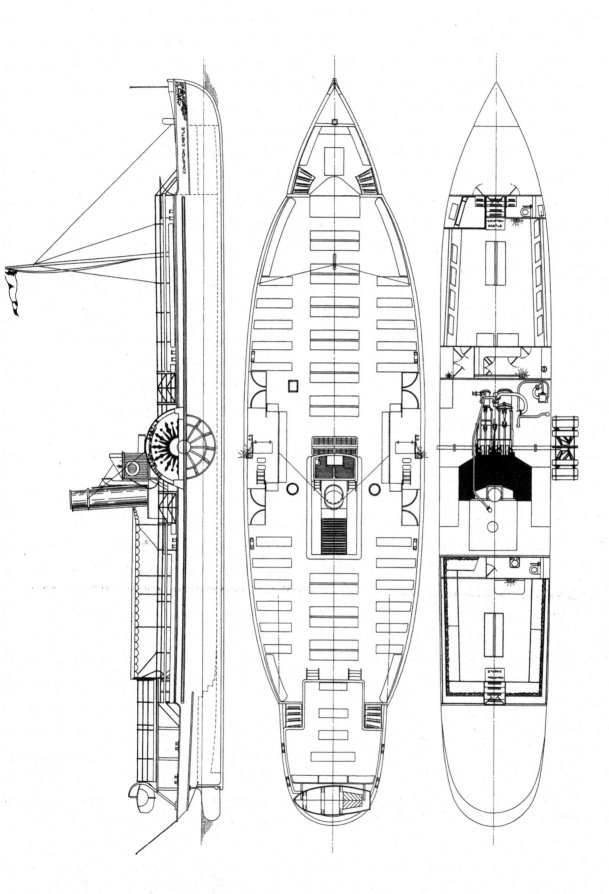

Fig 7.7 *A plan of the PS Compton Castle from Brian Moseley's book about the history of River Dart shipping.*

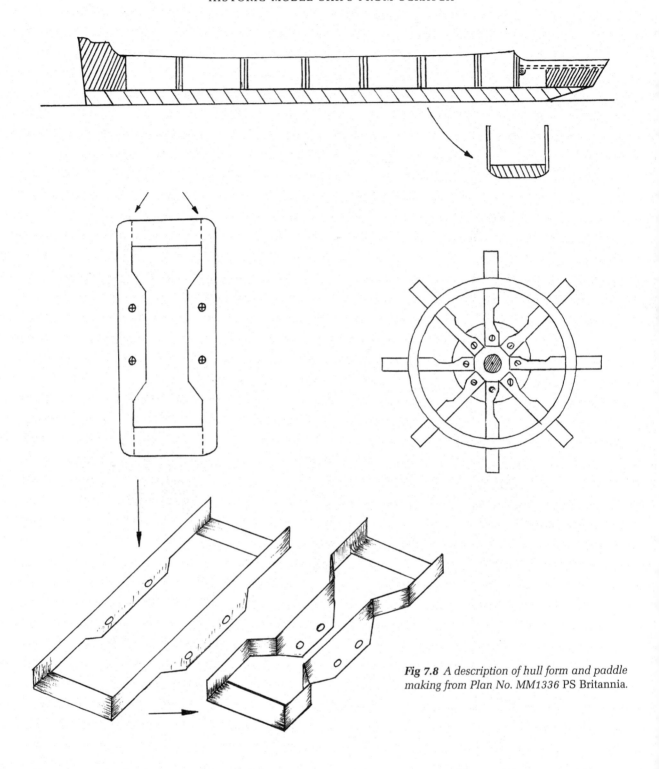

Fig 7.8 *A description of hull form and paddle making from Plan No. MM1336 PS Britannia.*

Building a paddle steamer

I shall not describe the whole process as most plans do this very well. However, it is interesting to note the few differences between conventional hulls and those of a paddle steamer.

Plan No. MM1336 *PS Britannia* built in Scotland 1896 and withdrawn from service 1956 is a good example of a large PS, 230ft long, 26ft 5in. beam, displacement 459 tons. She was P & A Campbell's original flagship.

The model is designed as a water model using a *Mamod* SE3 steam power unit. My model is a static one. At 43in. long she is quite large, but you could reduce this plan.

This is one of the hull types that lends itself to the slab-sided type of construction, see Chapter 10. Not many square frames are needed and the paddle wheels, cut in thin gauge sheet metal, will interest the model engineer. The drawings here show these interesting features of building a PS. The photographs of the completed model show you more detail. The paddle wheel drawings are not to scale and there are other ways of making the wheels, especially for those handy with a soldering iron.

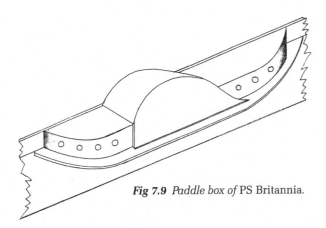

Fig 7.9 *Paddle box of* PS Britannia.

The first steamships

In 1802 an American named Fulton showed off a little vessel fitted with an 8 hp steam engine on the River Seine in Paris. In 1807 he made a larger vessel, the *Clermont*. This new boat sailed up the Hudson River with passengers and became the first commercially successful steamship to use paddles for propulsion.

Within three years Henry Bell began Britain's first steamship service on the Clyde.

In 1816 the first Channel crossing under steam took place. The *Elise* was a paddler of 70 tons and a little over 80ft long. It was very rough, taking over 18 hours to make the crossing. She steamed into Le Havre harbour and later steamed up the Seine to Paris.

In 1819 the American steam and sail paddle ship the *Savannah* made the Atlantic crossing. The novel ship could raise its paddle wheels to avoid drag

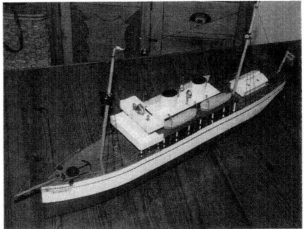

Fig 7.10 *The finished model of* PS Britannia *and a model of a gentleman's yacht, the* Boret.

when sailing. However, she could only carry a small amount of fuel and only steamed for about 80 hours of a journey that lasted an amazing 29 days!

8 'C' class destroyer and modern ships reflecting the past

HMS Chaplet

Most of the inspiration for models I have previously described date from before the 1900s so here is a small project for those interested in a more modern type of ship.

An acquaintance once served on *HMS Chaplet* during what was known then as the Cod War, when Iceland and Great Britain were at odds about fishing rights off Iceland. There had been a plastic kit of a 'C' class destroyer (now discontinued) but he had missed getting one at the time and was still very keen on finding a model of his old ship. He had an old photograph, this gave the profile of the ship and, of course, he had his memories. In *Jane's Fighting Ships* we found a very small line drawing, a plan view of the destroyer but there was nothing in the local library on this type of destroyer.

With tongue in cheek I said I would have a go, warning him that I really was not the best person to try to make something with so little reference. He agreed that a waterline model would be fine and you can see the results in the three photographs shown here. The mounting on a sea was my idea to avoid any problems with mounting the waterline model. See **Figs 8.2**, **8.3** and **8.4**.

It is a solid model and everything for it came from odds and ends in the workshop, with the exception of the patent modelling material for the sea which came from a local art shop.

Figs 8.2 and 8.3 HMS Chaplet, *close-up of centre section of the model.*

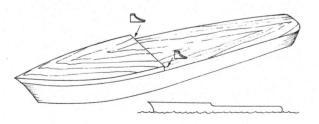

Fig 8.1 *Basic waterline hull, made from two pieces of planking horizontally glued, or the hull can be made in one piece with the break of deck cut down.*

The modelling material was knifed onto the raw wooden board and moulded with a round-ended spatula. Matt and semi-matt paints in blue, green and white with a touch of grey coloured the sea. The mounting board was edged and painted matt black.

The model had to be fairly small, measuring 15in. long. *Letraset* was used for the ship's number. The pylon mast was built up using split cocktail sticks and superglue. Multiple cannon barrels were made from small round panel pins and the funnel was shaped into an oval with boiling water, being a thin-walled plastic tube to start with.

Fig 8.4 The Chaplet *on a made-up sea mount. Artshop patent modelling medium used for the sea and painted in matt and semi-matt paints – blue, green, white and a little grey.*

It would have been nice to have had the benefit of a proper plan but my friend was delighted with the results and as an old model 'boatie' I was quite pleased.

The original boat ended up in the Pakistani Navy but is now broken up unfortunately – or perhaps fortunately.

Modern models lend themselves very well to the use of found objects, especially when working to a small scale. The hull of *Chaplet* was in two horizontally joined pieces cut on a band saw (see **Fig 8.1**)

and glued together. Being a small narrow solid hull and slab-sided except for the prow, those who have no band saw will not find it too difficult to shape with saw and plane.

Everything else was made up of small blocks of wood suitably shaped to the plan. The plan, incidentally, was a photocopy enlarged copy of a two and a half inch long plan drawing from *Jane's* as mentioned earlier. It looked a bit furry but was perfectly adequate for the outline plan. I did have the side view photo to go by. Note: the Nexus Plans Service can supply a huge variety of very good plans on warships from ironclads up to modern times. I found that making one of these wasn't as difficult as making, say, a frigate of 1805, so it is worth a try.

Modern sailing ships reflecting the past

There is a great deal of pleasure to be had by modelmakers in the ships that take part in various annual races like the Tall Ships race and Thames Barge races. Most of the barges are original or wrecks superbly rebuilt by enthusiasts.

The Tall Ships race is a much more robust race in the open sea needing extremely tough ships. The need for traditional fore and aft and square-rigged

Fig 8.5 This impression of the British-Australia Bicentennial Trust's schooner by English artist Arthur Saluz illustrates well a modern steel-hulled 35-metre schooner designed by Scottish-born naval architect and yacht designer, Colin Mudie. The ship was presented by Britain to mark the Australian Bicentenary in 1988. She was technically a brigantine but has been described as above (C.O.I. picture).

Fig 8.6 TS Royalist, *another beautiful modern ship designed by Colin Mudie, is a sail training brig made for the British Sea Cadet Corps. She was overall winner of the Tall Ships race in 1982 and 1983. This is certainly one of the models I would love to make (C.O.I. picture).*

craft has meant that modern designers have had to come up with modern versions of some of the old favourites.

I am always on the lookout for plans of some of these handsome ships – they are well worth looking for.

9 Ships' deck detailing

Apart from giving a model hull a fine and faithful shape, the detail you include on the deck of your model is one of the important features of modelmaking. There are many shops that stock useful items like ships' wheels, binnacles, gratings, airvents, chainplates and so on. It is up to you and your pocket whether you buy these parts or make them yourself from scratch or 'found objects' upon which you can perform a little surgery. Here are a few suggestions:

Chainplates
Copper wire of the large gauges. Hammer the tips of pieces to allow drilling through. Thin brass strip for the banded type.

Capstans
A number of found objects are useful – certain types of bottle caps, old wooden cotton reels, odd offcuts of dowel. Some types of waisted map pins for smaller vessels.

Airvents
A piece of brass or aluminium tube, topped with a wooden bead (homemade jewellery supply shop)

cut in half. You can also use plastic padding, shaped in a semi-dry condition, to top off the tube.

Gratings
You can buy very good ones from model shops, otherwise certain types of open-weave canvas and cotton can be purchased from stores dealing with

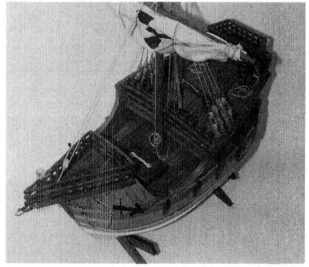

Fig 9.2 Catalan boat 1440.

Fig 9.1 British Revenue cutter 1763.

Fig 9.3 British trading cutter 1835.

Fig 9.4 British frigate 1824.

Fig 9.5 River Ouse barge 1840.

Fig 9.6 Passenger cargo ship 1930.

Fig 9.7 Trading cutter 1835.

Fig 9.8 Three-masted barque 1890.

Fig 9.9 Trading cutter 1835.

Fig 9.10 Paddle steamer 1925.

Fig 9.11 American pilot boat 1865.

Fig 9.12 Private steam yacht 1904.

Fig 9.13 *British channel packet 1833.*

carpet canvas. Children's large wool embroidery sheets in plastic and cross-stitch canvas are very good if painted and then mounted on a black card background.

Ships' wheels

These have always been a fiddly job to make yourself. The bought ones come in wood and in cast brass and as there is usually only one wheel on each model these are worth paying for. Some ships, of course, have gangs of two or four wheels.

A piece of dowel will serve as the centre of a homemade wheel, drilling the periphery and using copper or brass wire for the spokes radiating around the centre. Another ring of wire is soldered onto the spokes. The handle tips can be topped off with thin strips of sticky paper or you can dip the ends into PVA glue or old paint to form the handles when well dried.

Compass binnacles

Again a piece of brass tube or dowel topped off with an angled metal or plastic bead cut with a flat on one side and suitably painted.

Fig 9.14, 9.15, 9.16 *British barge 1920.*

Fig 9.17 *How to make your own blocks. Use a fine grain hardwood, walnut, lime, yew etc.*

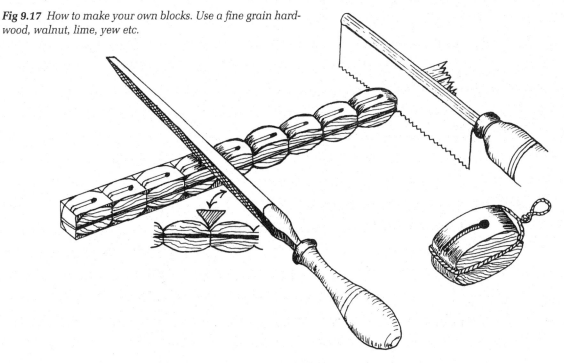

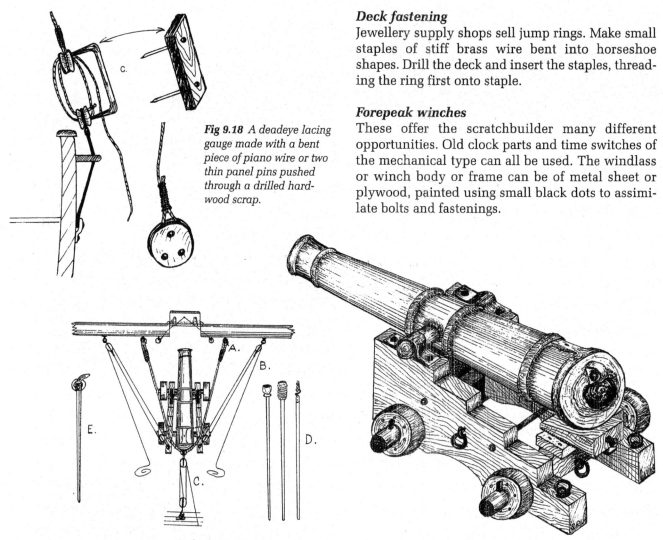

Deck fastening

Jewellery supply shops sell jump rings. Make small staples of stiff brass wire bent into horseshoe shapes. Drill the deck and insert the staples, threading the ring first onto staple.

Forepeak winches

These offer the scratchbuilder many different opportunities. Old clock parts and time switches of the mechanical type can all be used. The windlass or winch body or frame can be of metal sheet or plywood, painted using small black dots to assimilate bolts and fastenings.

Fig 9.18 *A deadeye lacing gauge made with a bent piece of piano wire or two thin panel pins pushed through a drilled hardwood scrap.*

Fig 9.19 *A standard ship's gun and carriage showing at A, B, C, D and E the breeching tackle, side and train tackle ropes and pulleys. Additional equipment is shown – ram rod, dampening mop, screw rod, for removing unfired charges and a lever bar with wheel to move the gun carriage. Good plans show gun positions.*

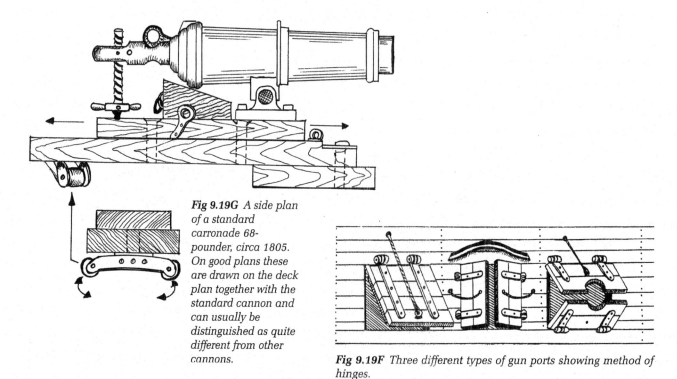

Fig 9.19G *A side plan of a standard carronade 68-pounder, circa 1805. On good plans these are drawn on the deck plan together with the standard cannon and can usually be distinguished as quite different from other cannons.*

Fig 9.19F *Three different types of gun ports showing method of hinges.*

Sail sheet horses

These are easily made from ⅟₁₆ or ⅛ metal rod bent suitably, fixed into a drilled deck and fastened with superglue.

Cannons

Here a convincing cannon or deck gun can be made from tapered dowel. Any thickened reinforcement on the barrel is built up with brown gummed paper. A small bead is stuck on the breech end for the bracing rope. The wooden carriage is made easily out of ply or thick card. When painted matt black the effect looks like metal. See any guns shown on model decks in this book– these were all made as

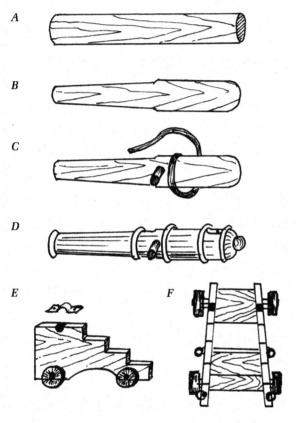

Fig 9.20 *A Start with a piece of dowel in the right scale. Cut to length of barrel.* **B** *Carve and taper barrel, sandpapering as you go.* **C** *Drill through side of barrel and push through a piece of solid rod, brass or steel (coathanger wire). This is the trunnion and fits a depression on the top edge of the gun carriage timber. A metal saddle usually bolted this down in place and can be made of thin sheet metal and stuck over with superglue. Gummed strip is rolled around barrel for thickening as indicated.* **D** *The completed barrel. When painting with matt or semi-matt black paint the raised gum strip collars soften out and look as one with the barrel. A small bead, stuck on the barrel end, completes the job.* **E, F** *The gun carriage can be fret-sawed out of thin ply. I have cut these on smaller versions from plastic coated card – this works well.*
Note: *The reinforcement rings around the barrel take only a few turns of thin gum strip. This is cut off, say, an 8in. length using a ruler and modelling knife. The thickness soon builds up. It is a method that can be used in many jobs when modelling a ship to assimilate metal rings and hoops on masts and yards. When painted they are completely convincing and save a lot of working time.*

described here. You can buy nice brass ones of course. See **Fig 9.20 A** to **F**.

Chains and turnbuckles

Homemade jewellery supply shops have a wealth of interesting items like chain and necklace screw fasteners, all in different sizes. My local shop also can supply all manner of cordage of the matt type for rigging (sold for bead threading).

Rigging cordage

I have a large supply of industrial button cord and carpet thread. Twist three or four strands together using a hand-twist drill and keeping it all taut, wipe the twisted strands under tension with PVA glue on a pad. Keep taut until dry. This makes very good main braces. Model shops have a good selection of rigging cord in different scales if you want the readymade rigging.

Blocks and pulleys

These essential items, made in wood and plastic, can be bought from specialist model shops. They come in many sizes and qualities. You can make them if time is not of the essence – the method is shown in *Model Ships from Scratch*. See **Fig 9.17**.

Deck cargoes on barges and traders

In the open holds of some model barges cargoes of stone, sand, gravel, timber, barrels and canvas trussed case can easily be made. Vermiculite, sold in plant shops, is mixed with *Polycell* to make gravel stones. Clippings from pruning make logs. Modelling clay makes small bricks – treat like pastry, roll out and cross cut with a knife. Macaroni, painted, makes convincing drainage pipes often carried by barges. A small wheelbarrow often found on barges can easily be made from scraps of offcut ply.

Portholes

Obviously washers of all sizes can be used, although the bought plastic variety do show small rivet bumps. A very small blip of glue left to dry on the washer and then painted can look like a bolthead or rivet.

Channel boards

These heavy boards, situated in line and aft of each mast, usually below or in line with the deck level, should be well glued and permanently nailed or pinned to the hull exterior. The chainplates rising from their fastenings lower down the hull are evenly spaced in the deep groove cut into the outside edge of each channel board. The edge is capped off with a strip of wood. See **Fig 9.25I**.

Ships' cannons

Fig 9.19 (from *Model Ships from Scratch*) is included for those who want to make their own ships' armaments. The plan of the gun's bracing is also shown.

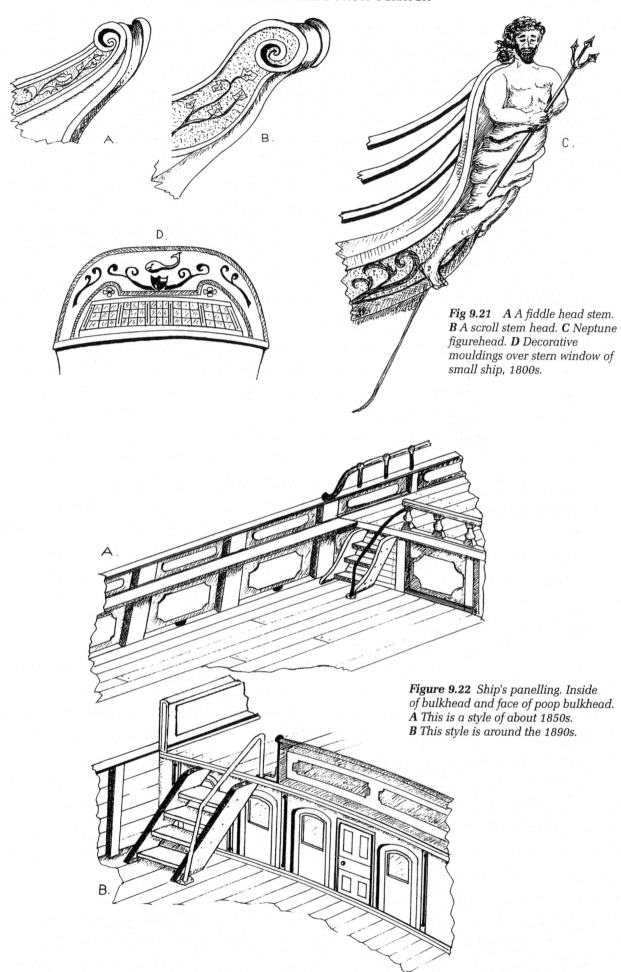

Fig 9.21 *A A fiddle head stem. B A scroll stem head. C Neptune figurehead. D Decorative mouldings over stern window of small ship, 1800s.*

Figure 9.22 *Ship's panelling. Inside of bulkhead and face of poop bulkhead. A This is a style of about 1850s. B This style is around the 1890s.*

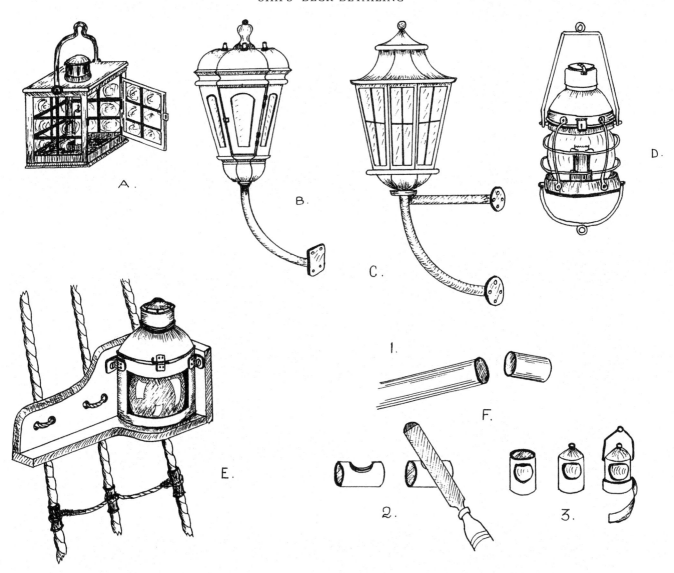

Fig 9.23 A *This stern lantern is a design described in the collection of the Maritime Museum in Barcelona. Candle-powered, it would have been used on the ships of Columbus' small fleet.* **B** *This is the kind of six-sided lantern with smoke vent pipes on its top found on ships of the late 1600s. Two or three were mounted over the stern of these well-decorated ships.* **C** *Here is the kind of six-sided lantern used on the sterns of ships in the 1790s. A simpler design to make than earlier types.* **D** *A brass ship's navigation lamp made by* Davey *of London. This kind of lamp, or similar types, were used over a long period during the late 1800s onwards. An upper and lower handle enabled the lamp to be lashed above with light chain or cable clips.* **E** *Another light by* Davey *is made of brass and copper. It is made as a port or starboard light. Two flat sides allow it to sit safely on the light screen. This illustration is for a port light. Oil-operated originally, these lamps were often altered for electric power after the early 1900s. Before these patent three-sided lights were made, an ordinary round lantern would have been used.* **F** *(1) Thin copper pipe cut into suitable lengths. (2) Half-round file used to make the window in lamp. (3) Plastic padding or plastic filler etc. used to make a conical lamp top, use bead as vent. To thicken the base of the lamp wrap sticky paper tape around base. Solder on handle after bending to shape. A dab of paint, white, red or green, inside the lamp will finish lamp – leave lamp natural colour or paint grey.*

The 3rd Rater described in Chapter 2 required 32- and 18-pounders, measuring about 2in. long overall, also 32-pounder carronades.

The ordinary cannons of 32- and 18-pounders were almost the same to look at with minor adjustments to the carriage steps and barrel thickness, so much so that it was hardly worth trying to show this minute difference.

The drawings show how, with the use of carving and brown gummed paper, you can make a convincing gun when painted matt or semi-matt black (see various deck views of the 3rd Rater in Chapter 2).

This standard type of cannon is shown in some detail because it was used over a very long period of history with hardly any noticeable change in its shape, and to a modelmaker it is a type that appears in many ships plans of Navy ships and East Indiamen.

Armament changed very little until the Navy introduced the carronade (named after its maker, the Carron Iron Foundry). This foreshortened, fat type of cannon, known as a 'smasher' appeared a little after 1779. Used in close encounters it fired a heavy shot with a smaller charge. The cannon balls

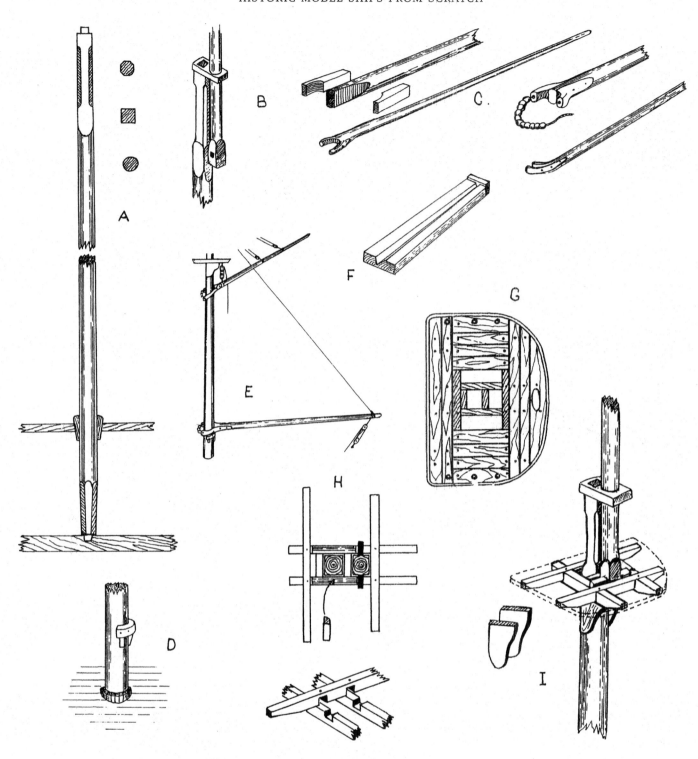

Fig 9.24 A Mast showing the method of shaping at the top where the round section goes into a square. **B** Main lower mast joins at the doubling with the top mast. Held by a mast cap at top. **C** Gaff poles and bottom booms of fore and aft sails. Method of making jaws on the thick end of each. **D** Jaw rest on mast to support boom end. **E** Gaff and boom as it is rigged before fitting sails. **F** A handy plank, V-cut and used for mast shaping and planing. **G** The planking plan for a top (this is the platform at the top of the lower mast). **H** The method of fixing crosstrees. These support the tops platform. **I** Cheeks or bibbs are fitted each side of mast to support crosstrees. The crosstrees form a frame that fits the top mast butt end. A fid pin stops the mast sliding through.

A note on mast and spar woods
On simple fore and aft sailers, masts can be made from bought dowels of different diameters. When dealing with masts that overlap at the doubling it is best to start with a length that has been squared up. This enables the top shaping of the mast with any carved flutes and squaring of the main lower masthead.

I find pine the best mast wood, the older the better. It should be bone dry and should split and plane very well. A grooved board with a stop is useful. See **Fig 9.24F**.

You can buy lengths of modelmakers' dowel in various woods ready to taper and shape if your hobby time is short.

I plane the squared up length taking off the four squared edges and so on until I have a rough round shape. The rest of the shaping is done with graded sandpaper. Top shaping with knife and files and any drilling completes the job.

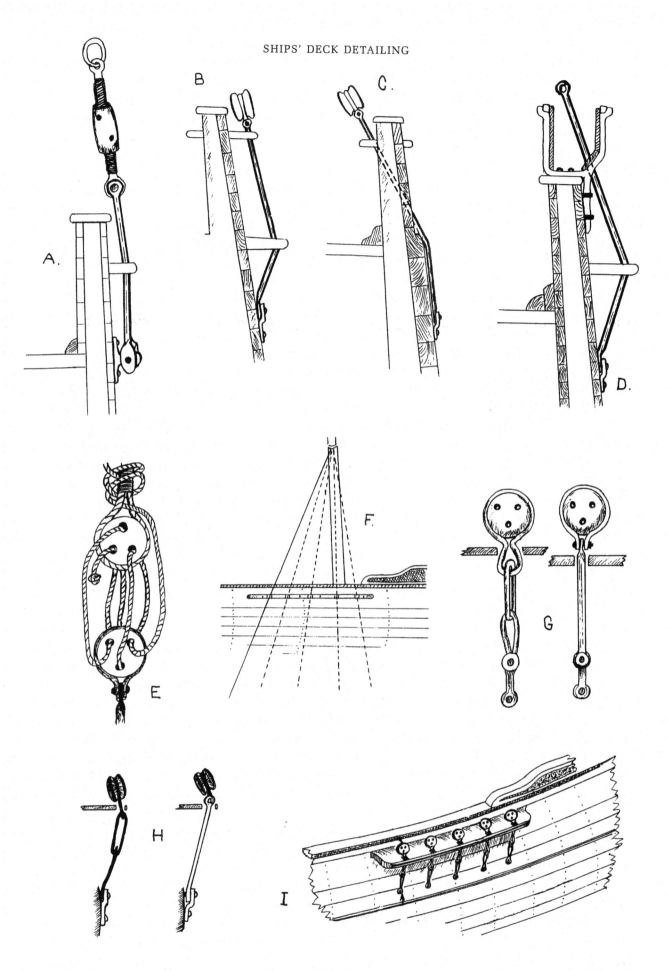

Fig 9.25 A to D *The four different methods of fixing chainplates to the hull. You may find slightly different methods on some plans.* **E** *The lanyard threading of shroud deadeyes.* **F** *Use cotton as a preliminary gauge to mark off the positions and angle of each shroud on the channel board before fitting shrouds.* **G & H** *Two different types of chainplates. Chain type and iron strap type.* **I** *Chainplates fitted through channel board, with lower deadeyes connected.*

were, in most cases, charged and fused and these exploded on impact causing much damage.

In the 1860s new types of breech-loading guns were being developed – see Chapter 5 **Fig 5.27**. Small calibre guns were mounted on the tops of fighting vessels for use when coming alongside the enemy, sometimes charged and loaded with grape shot. Large mortars were fitted to some ships with reinforced decks to fire up and over fortifications in coastal attacks. Ships called bomb ketches were designed for this type of gun.

Gun-port lids come in different styles as shown in **Fig 9.19F**. Hinges for the port lids can be bought from model shops and will save much time. Bolt

heads are usually cast into these and look more authentic than any you could make. They may not be functional and are used when port lids are shown closed.

Gun ports are usually shown on plans as a square with no detail so a little research may be necessary. It is an important detail and should not be skimped.

The tackle to control the gun is an important detail. Side tackle, train tackle and breeching ropes are shown in **Fig 9.19 A to E**.

The carronade is illustrated in **Fig 9.19G**. This gun had no conventional wheels except for a heavy castors at the rear end of the carriage. The illustration is of a 68-pounder circa 1805 – the year of

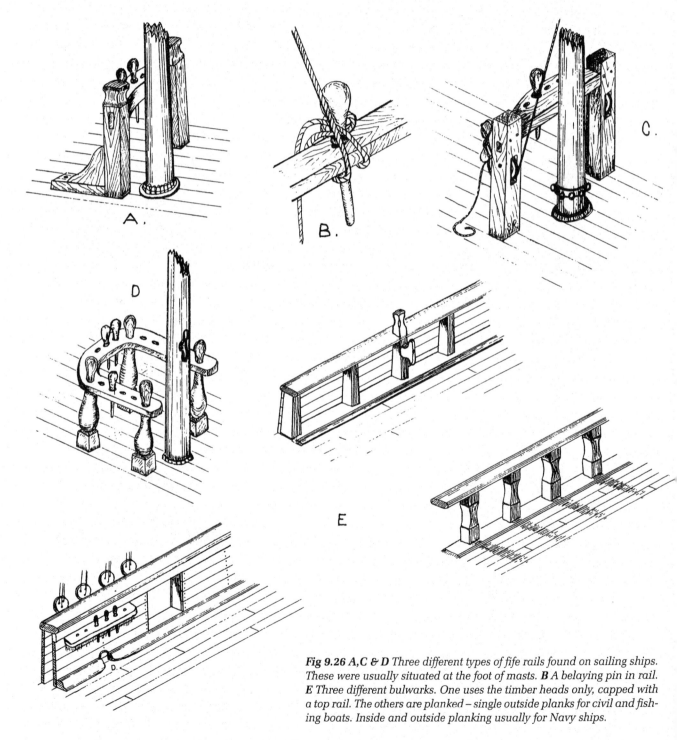

*Fig 9.26 A,C & D Three different types of fife rails found on sailing ships. These were usually situated at the foot of masts. **B** A belaying pin in rail. **E** Three different bulwarks. One uses the timber heads only, capped with a top rail. The others are planked – single outside planks for civil and fishing boats. Inside and outside planking usually for Navy ships.*

Trafalgar.

Decorative mouldings and figureheads

After the 1850s ship designs included less and less decorative embellishment. A little gingerbread (the gilded scrollwork and carving) is usually present on the stern and bows of ships like the *Cutty Sark* but nothing like that found on some East Indiamen of the 16th to 18th centuries. Spanish ships of this period had plenty – some, it could be said, were overloaded with gilded carving.

There are model shops that stock sets of moulded plastic ornamentation. This can be stuck on and gilded with a good quality light gold modelling paint. I have, in the past, found old goldleaf gilded picture frames beyond repair that can be recycled using pieces cut from the frame. Making your own decorations can be done using all manner of material. Modelling clay, some jewellery parts bought in hobby jewellery shops can be used, also semi-dry *Polyfilla*, plastic woods and wood fillers. This effort by designers in the 16th, 17th and 18th centuries to decorate, in most cases adding useless weight to a vessel, was replaced by improving the internal finish of woodwork, especially on civilian vessels of

the late 1800s. Good panelling between fluted timberheads and panelled doors in panelled bulkheads at break of the poop deck made for quite a homely environment for civilian passengers travelling on these ships. See **Fig 9.22**. All this gives the modelmaker plenty of enhancing detail to think about – this is not always indicated on the plan.

Windows, doors, protective wooden rails and stairways up to the poop can all be made with mild forms of decoration depending, of course, on the exact period of the ship you are making and its size. There are quite a few types of material you can use for this listed below:

- Soft wires
- Sheet card
- Thin ply $\frac{1}{32}$in. and $\frac{1}{16}$in.
- Sheet plastic $\frac{1}{32}$in. and $\frac{1}{16}$in.
- Decorative gilt chain
- Patent modelling medium
- Plastic wood
- *Polyfilla*

Figureheads

These can be divided into the inanimate and the living, humans and animals, busts or whole figures.

Fig 9.27 A A stern davit. Usually the Captain's gig was hung on these. B Boom davits, hinged on bulwarks opposite the mizzen mast shroud channels. Ships' boats like pinnaces or whalers were slung from this type of davit. C A davit of about 1860 onwards (similar to modern davits). D The catting gear for the anchor hangs from a kind of davit near the bow of a ship. This equipment is usually referred to as the 'catheads'.

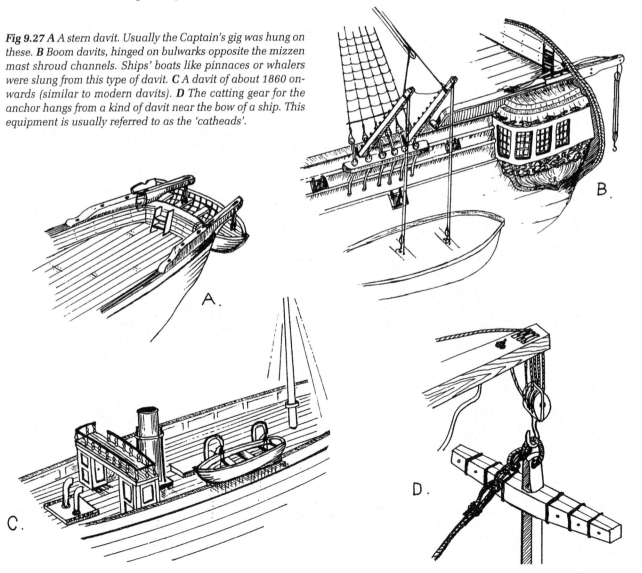

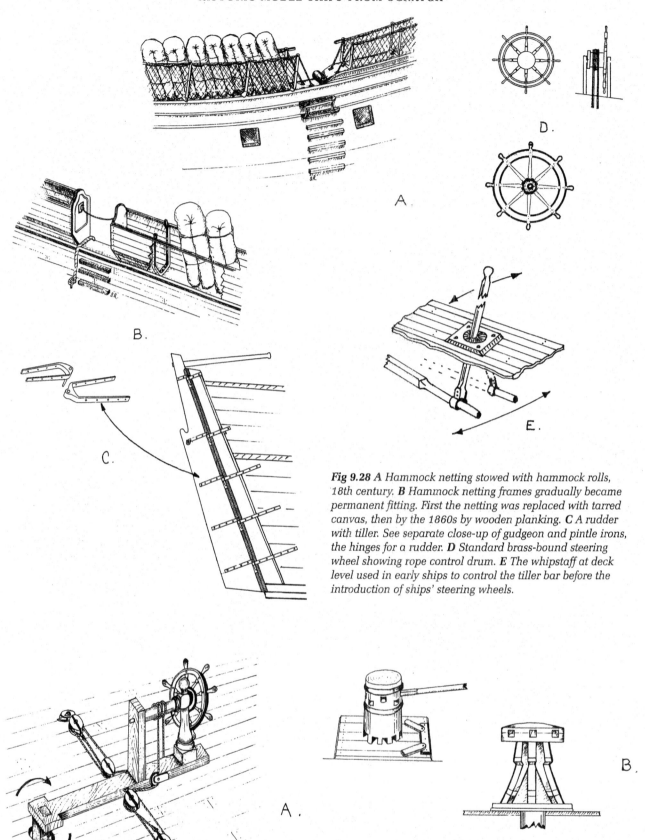

Fig 9.28 A Hammock netting stowed with hammock rolls, 18th century. **B** Hammock netting frames gradually became permanent fitting. First the netting was replaced with tarred canvas, then by the 1860s by wooden planking. **C** A rudder with tiller. See separate close-up of gudgeon and pintle irons, the hinges for a rudder. **D** Standard brass-bound steering wheel showing rope control drum. **E** The whipstaff at deck level used in early ships to control the tiller bar before the introduction of ships' steering wheels.

Fig 9.29 A Many different ways of connecting the steering wheel power to the rudder through a tiller bar were employed. Here the steering wheel drum and tiller bar are on the deck top. The bar and wheel assembly moves when the wheel is turned. Capital ships' pulley gear was under the deck and the ship's wheel and drum above deck. **B** Two different capstans. A simple log type used in the early 16th century. The other is a type found on ships of the late 1700s onwards. Made of hard wood and sometimes metal bound. Many of the larger ships had them joined on the same vertical core. One on top deck connected to the one on the deck below. The ship's cable would come in on the lower deck and was connected to the lower capstan. Working in this way, two capstan crews could supply many pairs of hands to the capstan bars at the same time on different decks.

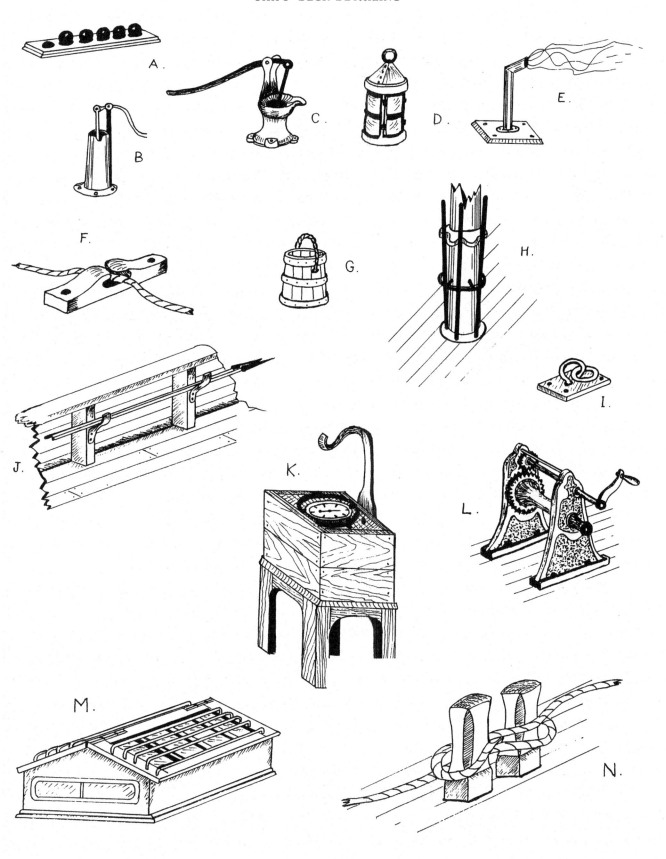

Fig 9.30 A *A shot garland found around gratings or at the foot of bulwarks near gun positions. Shot in various sizes from shotgun cartridges make good cannon balls!* **B** *A type of deck mounted pump.* **C** *A larger type of pump for bilge water.* **D** *A deck lantern.* **E** *Galley smoke stack.* **F** *A fair lead found on the bulwark top or on deck.* **G** *A cooper-made deck bucket.* **H** *A mast rack for stowing capstan bars or battle pikes.* **I** *A ring bolt mounted at deck level.* **J** *Another type of rack for holding pikes or other types of long gear.* **K** *A wooden compass box with non-ferrous lamp hook.* **L** *An iron geared winch, circa 1890.* **M** *Skylights with protective bars over glass lights. These would open for fine weather.* **N** *Deck-mounted bitts usually situated in pairs at bows and sterns, both sides of the deck.*

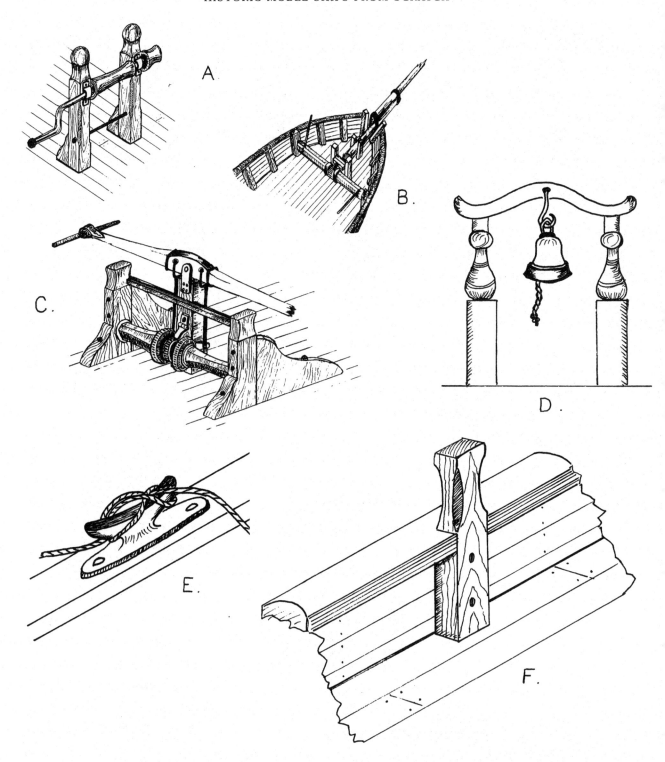

Fig 9.31 A *A simple direct hand winch. This type usually at base of mast or near small hatch, used for light loading jobs.* **B** *A log-type windlass found on cutters in the late 1700s. It used the two bow timber heads to support each end of the drum. Double bitts at the end of the bowsprit formed part of the windlass giving an attachment for the ratchet arm.* **C** *A double-armed pump action wind-lass found on larger ships of the 1800s.* **D** *A ship's bell. This was situated at various places on a deck. Look at your plan. This bell frame is designed to act as a boom rest in smaller ships.* **E** *A cleat, made originally of hardwood but later of metal. The rope is in a 'by-the-wind' hitch.* **F** *A bitt formed at the top of an extended timber head.*

The stemhead usually supports these. As time and the design of ships moved on the stemhead became less upright. The clipper-type stemhead was becoming almost horizontal and any figurehead took on an almost flying position tucked under the root of the bowsprit. Some ironclads had large cast iron ram bows, usually in the form of a crest.

Soldier types, Neptune, lions and various female forms were used as subjects for figurehead treatment. From the mid-19th century , colouring for the ladies was usually white with low neckline, diaphanous dresses, coloured hemlines, coloured hair and flesh tones. Before this time highly coloured figureheads predominated with red, green and blue with gilt yellow and red for the wild beasts.

Fiddlehead stems and scroll stems bore carving on the sides. The scroll curled down, the fiddlehead curled up. See **Fig 9.21 A** and **B**. These scrolls took the place of figureheads on minor ships. Again figureheads can be bought, but there are so many small model toys now like soldiers and female forms in the right scale that with a little surgery can be made into figureheads.

Steering gear and rudders

Steerboards were the first method of steering a large boat (starboard side). They were situated near the stern of the vessel. Like a broad oar, it hung at about 70° and was lashed or held in a stirrup block and was manipulated by 13th-century helmsmen.

In the 14th century, the vertical rudder mounted on the sternpost with pintle pins dropping into gudgeons became the method. The rudder was controlled by a tiller fixed to the head of the rudder. The tiller position was usually exposed to the weather. In the 15th century the tiller was operated from under the poop deck. Later, in the 16th century, a kind of cockpit enabled the helmsman to operate from above the tiller with the aid of a vertical steering bar, a whipstaff, attached to the tiller arm and ending through the deck in the cockpit. His vision for steering was much improved. See **Fig 9.28 C** and **E**.

In the 17th and 18th centuries the ship's wheel developed, operated with ropes and pulley, sometimes under the deck steering position. Wheels on large ships were sometimes 6ft in diameter and in gangs of two or four enabling many pairs of hands to hold the ship's direction in very heavy weather.

Steering gear is usually noted on model plans.

Hammock nettings

From the late 1700s, iron frames supporting net-like baskets were positioned along the ship's mid section and the poop rail. These were used as stowage places for sailors' hammock rolls, providing a padded protection from musket balls and wood splinters in battle. These are an important detail to show in ships of Nelson's time. They developed into permanent boxes on ships of the mid-1800s. See **Fig 9.28 A** and **B**. In this drawing (**A**) is shown the nettings of 1800 and (**B**) is how they looked in the 1860s.

10 Systems of hull building – half-block models and the mounting of models

The making of a correct and shapely hull is, to some modelmakers, one of the hardest parts of the hobby. For those with a workshop, the solid form of hull is probably the best to start with. There is usually a collection of offcuts to be found knocking about. If mistakes are made it's not an expensive exercise to try again.

Those modelmakers without a workshop bench to carve out a shape from a block of wood will find it easier to cut out frame bulkheads from thin ply-wood and set up a model on the kitchen table. It's rather like making model flying aircraft except that we clad it with thin planks and not tissue paper.

The bread-and-butter or sandwich form of construction falls between the two methods described above. When the various layers are cut to their profile size and layered together, the shape of the hull starts to emerge. The final shaping is not quite as hard as carving a shape from a square block. The different ways of building are listed below and the various drawings will help with the written details.

Fig 10.1 A Revenue cutter under construction. Carvel-laid planks are glued to frames then pinned until dry.

Solid carved hulls

Small hulls can be made from a single block of wood, while the larger ones can be made from layers or blocks glued and cramped together. See **Fig 10.12A**.

A bread-and-butter or sandwich construction

These hulls are made (usually indicated on a plan) from six to eight layers of wooden planking. These are graded in size when cut to the plan profile. The inside area of each plank is cut out and then all planks are glued together. The stepped shape outside of the planks is then planed and shaped. The inside steps can be left. See **Fig 10.10**.

Plank on frames

This is the way most of us think about hull building and is the way the real boats are made. Most plans are for carvel planking i.e. one plank tightly placed against the next. See **Fig 10.11 B** and **C**.

Clinker-built hulls

This type of building is seldom found in model plans as they can be quite difficult to construct. Here the planks overlap one another. Viking long ships, Norfolk wherries and some ships' boats are clinker constructed. There are enough carvel-built model plans to last most people a lifetime unless you want to try your hand. Many of the smaller British working boats were clinker built – these are well described in Eric McKee's *Working Boats of Britain* (Conway Publications).

There is a fifth way to construct a hull used by the shipwrights of old to plan the massive timbers of the barrel-shaped hulls, see **Fig 10.9**. This is not some-

Fig 10.2 The cutter being rigged.

Fig 10.3 The Revenue cutter (circa 1760) finished and rigged with sails. Deck cannons shown in firing position.

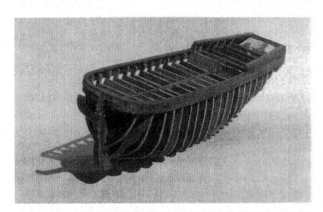

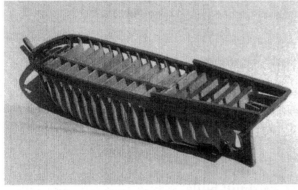

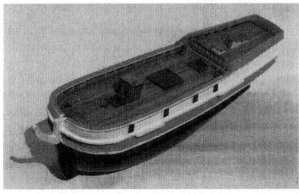

Fig 10.4 to 10.6 The progression of constructing a plank-on-frame model. An 1820s brig.

thing the average modelmaker should undertake. You can see some of these models in the Christies maritime sales catalogue and they fetch very high prices as being the ultimate in the modelmaker's craft. Some planking is usually missing to show off the framing within the hull.

The system of building up the frames is exactly what it would be in reality. The old shipmakers relied on grown shapes in the various timbers they needed. In fact this was so important that large wooden templates were taken into the oak forests and placed against growing trees until they found the right curve or shape, for instance, where a branch bent out from the main trunk of a tree. See Chapter 2 **Fig 2.23**.

These trees were marked by the buyers of the timber and when cut they were delivered to the shipyards for further shaping and joint cutting.

To undertake a model like this may be out of the question, but you could try a cross-section model including the fully rigged mast etc. In this way you can show all the decks and guns in position – a real challenge but a very interesting exercise. See Chapter 2 **Fig 2.26**.

Slab-side hull building

Here is an idea I have used on hulls like barges, paddle steamers and some straight-sided steamers that need to be hollow inside.

If the thought of a lot of carving puts you off, here is a quick way of avoiding it. Look at your plan, especially the chine curve. Use a base plank with sufficient thickness to allow for the maximum curve. Plywood is used to bridge the centre section between two blocks of soft wood at bow and stern. This system is particularly useful with bluff-bowed models or modern steamer hulls, see **Fig 10.8**, where planking or carving might prove difficult. The size of the blocks of wood to be used each end will depend on the degree of stern and bow profile shape. Avoid nailing the ply to the blocks and use a good PVA glue. After any filling needed, apply two or three coats of paint, you will be surprised with the results.

You can only get away with this system on a few types of models.

Tools for the job

Any handyman will find some of the tools needed in his tool box, like small planes, saws, chisels, files, rasps and drills. There are a few you might have to buy that will make modelling a little easier.

Pin vices are usually hand operated. They consist of a metal rod, usually milled for grip, topped with a small drill chuck. This I find invaluable to hold very small drill bits for piercing yards and masts and any other jobs needing a very small hole. Any good tool shop can supply these – buy at least two so you don't have to keep changing drill bits.

A **pointed steel rod** mounted in a wooden handle. This is tapered to a very sharp point, about $\frac{1}{16}$in. diameter rod will do. This is used to open up some holes already drilled or to prick planks lightly to place small nails into before knocking in.

A **set of small files**. Half-round, flat, triangular 'V' shapes and round are very useful. The 'V' types are for grooving handmade blocks etc.

Small-backed saw. Sold in model shops – or a small fine **dovetail saw**.

Frame saws. These can be like the old hand fretsaw or a jeweller's saw, as long as you can fit metal fret blades into the saw.

Vibro fretsaws. Most useful but not essential. These take standard fret blades, as above, but can be expensive. Electrically operated, the prices are around £50 to £90.

Knives. The scalpel-type handle with various fitting blades and a *Record* or *Arrow* type handy knife with retracting blade is a must.

Small draw knife. You may find these difficult to come by. I have one made from an old 12in. file by the local blacksmith. You can buy them but they might be a little too big. The draw knife is used for roughing out a block for a solid model. It is like using a plane but the angle of cut is controlled by your own hands. It needs practice and you can easily over-cut what you really want.

Hammers. A small size ball-pein hammer and a very small hammer (toffee hammer type) should be in your kit of tools.

A **small soldering iron** for the non-ferrous metal parts you make.

Small bench vice – this is very useful to grip various things when cross-cutting or filing metal etc. Also essential are a few different types of tweezers.

Brushes for painting the model need to be in sizes you feel happy with. Nos 0, 1 and 2 sizes for detail painting in situ, larger ones, both flat and pointed, for other jobs like hull painting.

Note: I have a small bandsaw which saves time when you want to cut the prow and stern taper shape from a solid block before you carve it, but this is not essential – hand sawing can be used for this job. If you have a little money to spare, there are a number of small woodworking power-operated machines like small circular saws, pillar drills, bandsaws and flex drive drills with over a hundred different tools to fit the drive made by *Dremel*. Again not essential – I don't possess one yet.

I have not mentioned clips to hold some parts or planks in place, especially when gluing the bulwark planks to the timber heads. Bulldog clips and clothes' pegs are very useful. Small modelmaker 'G' clamps are another type that are helpful with some jobs.

You can always improve on your tool collection as long as it isn't a fad.

Half models

This is a method of taking off lines but is not something you would need to do very often, if at all. Good shipwrights' half models are rare as most of them are mounted on boards and hang on the walls of yacht clubs and boating enthusiasts' homes. These were originally used by boatbuilders in the old days and were very often the only item they worked from (no computer-aided graphics!).

It is possible to take off the measurements and build a model and I have included details of this system for those with a technical interest in such problems. I will describe one way of doing this but there may well be other systems.

It is rather like tapping your head with one hand and rubbing your stomach with the other, but the gadget described below will work once you get the hang of it. See **Fig 10.7**.

1 Use a piece of good drawing paper.
2 Draw a base line parallel to the bottom edge of the paper. Draw vertical station lines, usually about twelve at right angles.
3 Lay the model flat-side down on the paper base line, lining it up with the keel if it is parallel with the load waterline.
4 If the keel is not parallel with the load line place the model with the LWL parallel to the

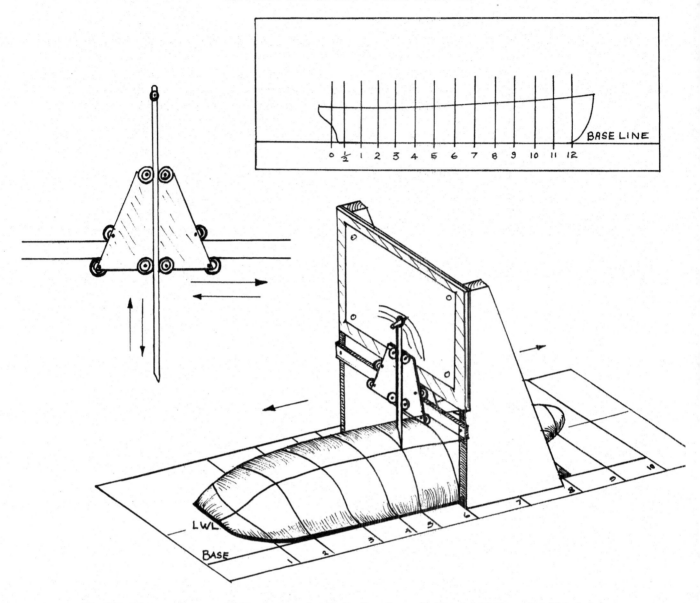

Fig 10.7 *A homemade gauge that you can use to take the lines from a half model. Not to scale in this drawing.*

Fig 10.8 *Slab-sided construction, suitable for a few types of hull. Paddle steamers, some cargo boats and barges.*

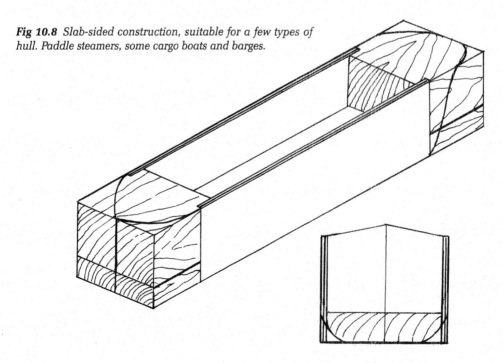

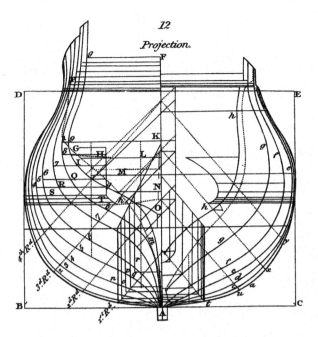

Fig 10.9 Cross section, frame plan. A ship of the late 1700s.

Fig 10.10 Bread-and-butter or sandwich construction is often indicated on plans for sailing models like the schooner Julia May. Nexus Plans Service Plan No. MM1324. It will give you a hollow hull and if you use a waterproof glue when sticking the layers together, a strong leakproof hull. The cross section shown at (A) has had the outside shaped but the inside left stepped. To lighten the hull remove the steps and paint well inside if you are going to float it. The number of laminations will be indicated on the plan. Hulls with acute convex and concave shapes will mean a greater number of layers. Julia May has seven layers, each about twelve millimetres thick. C shows the inside area of one of the laminations removed.B shows a set of six laminations and D is a larger vessel with different decks and a greater number of laminations.

base line.

5 Draw around the model carefully. This will give you the bow, stern and sheer shape. Remember when placing the model down to arrange it so that the station lines on the paper fall where you want them in relation to the model. See drawing Station 5 or 6 being about the middle of the model length.

Making the drawing gauge

I am not an engineer so I used wood and some metal for this little project. The gauge size depends on the size of the model. The mechanism has to fit over the model so no measurements are shown in the drawings and it is not to scale. If the half model is polished, cover each station with masking tape to avoid scratching the surface of the model.

This way of taking off the measurements was shown to me many years ago and I have only tried it once so I am not an expert.

The small wheels run on the rail bar giving a two-way horizontal movement. The wheels that grip the vertical gauge, topped with a pencil stub, move up

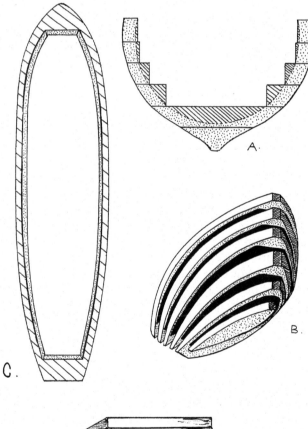

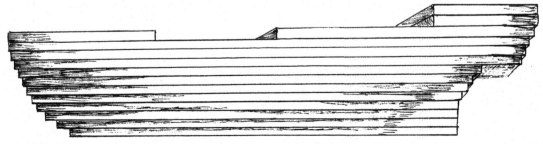

and down. I seem to remember at the time removing the wheels of one of my son's small cars for the vertical gauge wheels. When the tyres were removed the groove fitted the up and down gauge very well. The vertical board takes the paper, this is pinned to the board. The model must not move while the cross sections are being taken off. The success of the operation depends on how well you have made the apparatus – an extra hand in the form of a friend may be of assistance.

Building a plank-on-frame model

As most of the plans available deal with the above method of construction it is worth spending some time discussing this.

Regarding your plan, if it is to the size you want the finished model to be then you can start, but should it need to be reduced then this can be done on a photocopier at your local copying shop. Make very sure that you use the same degree of enlargement or reduction on every plan, needless to say.

Getting the plan lines for the cross-section stations from the plan on to wood can be done in a number of ways:

1 By tracing off, then sticking the tracing on to your wood ready to cut or fretsaw out.
2 Using carbon paper under the plan and with a stylus press through onto the actual sheet of wood or onto another paper that can then be cut and stuck onto the sheet wood.

Whichever way you use be very accurate – it is at this early stage that everything can go wrong.

Numbers are usually noted on each frame on the plan. If they are not, then number them yourself. Transfer the numbers to each frame/bulkhead that you cut out. Decide from the beginning to cut on the line or the outside of the traced line – whichever you choose, stick to the same for every bulkhead.

Before you cut out anything you must decide whether you need to include the timberheads within the top part of each bulkhead. You may choose not to at this stage, but add them as individual pieces later to the bulkhead top.

You will have to draw in the slots to come out of the bulkheads. These are at the keel position of each bulkhead, see **Fig 10.11B**. Sometimes the design will need a slot cut in the top of the bulkhead to receive a deck beam.

Making the keel, stempost and sternpost comes next. This is the backbone for the bulkhead frames to be attached. See **Fig 10.11B**.

Here again great caution is needed when setting bulkheads to the keel. The slots cut in the bulkhead should fit tight onto the keel but not have to be forced into position. This will cause distortion.

It is best to fit every bulkhead onto the keel then the central deck beam, if one is fitted. Do not glue anything at this stage. Look down the assembled structure. Place it on the plan to make sure everything is in the right place, slight adjustments can be made before gluing. It is not necessary to disassemble – simply squirt your PVA glue or superglue over the connecting parts of the structure and wait for it to dry. The glue will seep into joints and when dry will be quite firm.

Planking

This wood can be bought in mainly two colours, light and dark. The light is usually lime wood, the dark can be made of a number of woods including walnut and some mahogany types. The method with small models is to glue the plank onto the frames and pin until dry. Planks can be bought in all sizes so choosing the right scale of plank for your model is important. I find it useful to have a bundle of 2mm × 6mm and 2mm × 4mm lime strip planking always in my stock of materials – this size will fit a wide variety of models.

Some modelmakers like to see the ship's fastenings in a model, so nail heads should show. Small 7mm brass nails can be bought but I find these difficult to use and tweezers will be necessary. Most of my models that are carvel-planked do not show nail heads – the planks present a smooth finish that looks fine when filled and painted. See Chapter 5 **Figs 5.4** and **5.5**.

Make sure you lay the planks on alternate sides and that at bow and stern the edges of the bulkheads are shaved to fit the curve taken by the plank. See **Fig 10.11D**. I find it best to first fix a plank along both sides in a position about two plank widths down from the deck line. Do this with the hull keel up.

The bending of planks can be helped if a little heat can be applied to the planks at the bow and where it rounds down towards the stern. Use a medium soldering iron and rub the plank while you gently bend it upwards, hold for a second or two then it will set the curve. Warm water or steam are other methods of bending. This takes longer as a board with two-inch nails knocked in vertically is used to set the bend after dampening the planks. Leave to dry before applying glue. Many of my models have been made without the use of heat- or water-assisted bending – much depends on the hull shape and the thickness of planks. The sheer of the bulwark top above deck level may need shaped edges to the plank. Some foredecks and poop decks will need extra short lengths of planking as these areas rise above the centre deck level. Leave this as the last planking job. The timberheads that rise from the frame above deck level supply the support for the side bulwarks. These are either cut in as part of the frame/bulkhead or attached as vertical pieces glued to the bulkhead frames and come up above the deck level. The exterior planking around stem and stern may need tapering due to any concave or convex curve of the hull. It is best, I find, to present

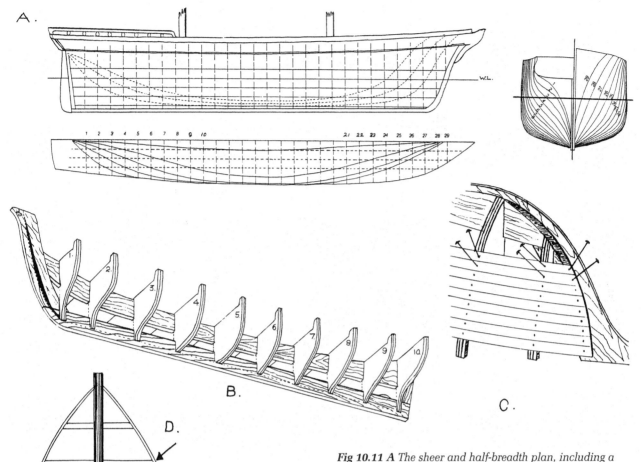

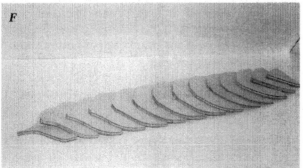

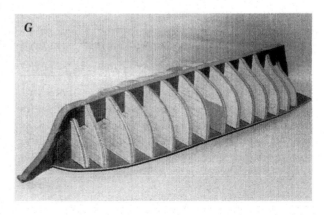

Fig 10.11 A *The sheer and half-breadth plan, including a body cross-section plan of a two-masted sailing ship. The various cross-section stations are numbered on most plans you buy.* **B** *After cutting out, the various frames are fitted to the keel and in some cases a central deck beam.* **C** *The bow of a plank-on-frame model. The prow piece is grooved to receive the plank end – these are glued and pinned in position until dry. The shape of the hull usually dictates the order of planking. Plank on alternate sides to avoid the hull twisting.* **D** *Make sure that the frame edges are shaved at bow and stern to allow a good fit for the planks.* **E** *If you are using paper templates for the individual bulkhead frames, it is best to use Polycell type wallpaper paste to fix them on to your ply pieces. It is very effective and saves using proper glue.* **F** *The bulkhead frames after cutting out. In this case, because the model is a larger type, quarter-inch thick ply was used.* **G** *Frames attached and glued to the keel piece. In this case the keel is quite deep to give strength to the model and the attached frames. In this picture the underdeck of ⅛in. ply has been fixed to the frame heads. Planks will eventually be laid onto this deck base.*

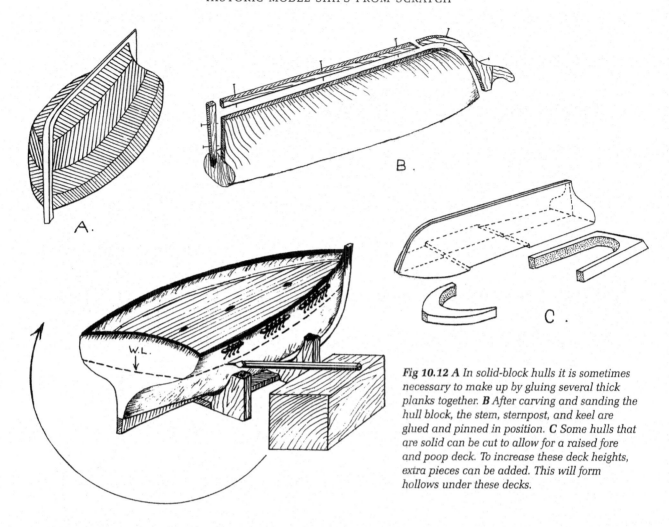

Fig 10.12 A *In solid-block hulls it is sometimes necessary to make up by gluing several thick planks together.* **B** *After carving and sanding the hull block, the stem, sternpost, and keel are glued and pinned in position.* **C** *Some hulls that are solid can be cut to allow for a raised fore and poop deck. To increase these deck heights, extra pieces can be added. This will form hollows under these decks.*

a plank up to this run of strakes, pin it and pencil or mark the plank edge in some way. Unpin and cut to shape, re-present the plank then glue and pin it. When planking reaches the keel and is finished you can go back to the bulwark rise above deck level and plank this, paying attention to the sheer curve and cutting the planks accordingly.

Filling in any cracks can be done with *Polyfilla* or a good quality stopping paste, like *Brummer* stopping. Lightly rub down the planked hull at this stage and when you are satisfied there are no dips and bumps give it a sealing coat of white or grey undercoat.

Other hull materials

To the purist, making a model ship hull from anything but wood is out of the question, but for some modellers it is a way to start. *Maritime Models of Greenwich*, who deal exclusively with model ships and boats, have a selection of seventy different hulls moulded in styrene or glass fibre. This would certainly give you a head start if the carving or planking of a model has deferred you from starting. You would still be making the rest from scratch!

Hull painting and finishing

I am often asked "What colour shall I paint my finished model? What colour should it be below the waterline etc?". Here again a good plan will indicate these important details. As to a ship's bottom, much depends on the period. All kinds of mixtures to prevent rotting and the dreaded teredo worm burrowing into ships' keels and planks have been used. Lead sheet was too heavy so coppering with sheets of thin copper was introduced by the Navy in 1761. The frigate *Alarm* was treated with this method. Iron bolts used in construction had to be changed to copper because the galvanic action caused between iron bolts and copper sheeting had a serious effect. All ships in the Navy had to obey the 1783 order to change to copper bolts below the waterline. Prior to coppering, layers of tar-impregnated canvas were sandwiched between two layers of boards. So here we have black bottoms, shiny copper bottoms and, in ships from 1490s, white bottoms until around the mid 1600s according to contemporary models. In very early ships self-coloured timbers with no paint seems to be the bottom colour.

The insides of bulwarks in warships on top decks and between decks have been painted red for obvious reasons -- this was eventually changed to white.

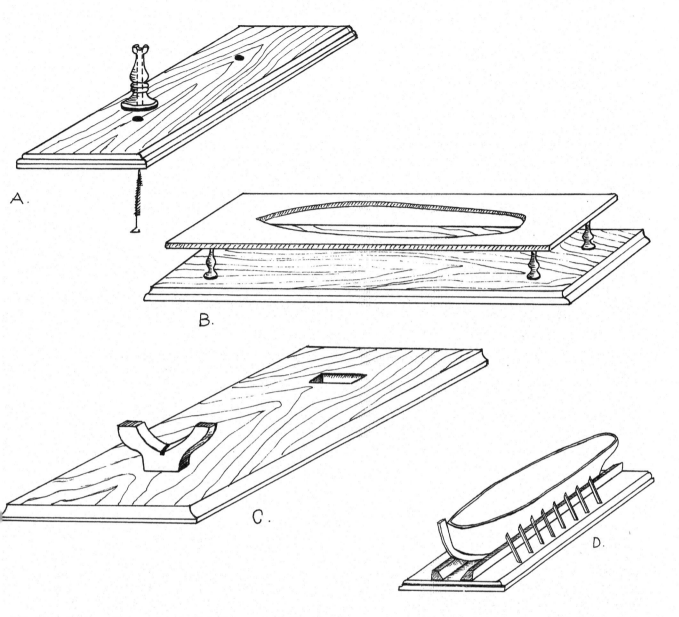

Fig 10.13 A A turned brass column with hollow centre, held in place by a wood screw. The screw goes into the model hull about half an inch. *B* A yacht mount. The raised platform has a profile hole cut into it, its column support thus allowing a deep keel hull to sit comfortably. *C* A cradle piece made of wood is glued into the base board or it can be simply glued flush and screwed from below. *D* A mount built as a slipway stock gives a sense of reality to any model.

Wooden rails were usually left natural, some oiled, some varnished. In Drake's time chequered multi-colours were all the rage. Gilding or gingerbread work was common on warships and East Indiamen. In the Navy this gilding and fancy carving was paid for by the richer captains of war vessels (a strange practice) – a kind of 'one upmanship' between captains of the fleet!

Masts were usually left natural on working boats while warships had painted masts. In Nelson's time every ship seemed to be a mustard yellow and black like the *Victory* is painted today. The iron bands around these masts were painted black. Some natural coloured masts were painted in the doubling, where main and top masts were joined – perhaps this helped seamen at night.

The ships mentioned earlier with white bottoms seemed to have much of the timber left natural, except perhaps their forecastles and poop deck bulwarks which were coloured with bright colours in Elizabethan times.

If you are uncertain about colours do a little research. I am always guided by the plans or by contemporary models which are usually dated. These are sometimes on view in museums such as the Science Museum or the Maritime Museum at Greenwich.

Note: thin copper sheet pieces or sheet for cutting are available in some model shops should you want to try coppering your model's bottom. Stained glass hobby shops sell adhesive copper foil on rolls.

Paint

Most model shops, whether they deal in model ships or not, will have model paints in a whole range or colours. Glossy, matt and semi-matt egg-shell finishes in all colours can be bought.

The bottoms of ship models are usually painted matt or semi-matt. I keep black, copper colour and white in my workshop. Other useful colours are grey, beige, yellow, dark blue, light blue and red.

Varnish – the semi-matt type – is useful on masts, booms and yards. These I usually lightly stain before varnishing as most wood looks too pale. I like to aim for a weathered look. The centre sections of yards are sometimes coloured white or grey where they are in contact with the mast, the rest is left natural. Cannons or guns are semi-matt black like most of any other iron or metal work on deck. Winches and anchors are the same.

Mounting model ships

Not many models will stand unsupported with the exception of perhaps a barge. A well-finished mount can be a work of art in itself as some museum pieces show. The bulk of some models will need a fairly substantial mount while the finer hulls can be given the delicate treatment. Some yachts with a deep keel will need a special mount.

Added interest can be given to some models by displaying them on working stocks, as if they were finished and ready to launch.

Professionally made cases for models can be incredibly expensive but making them yourself is fine if you feel confident. In Chapter 5, **Fig 5.28** (photo) shows a modern plastic case made professionally – the model was very long and a real glass case would have made it much too heavy. In Chapter 7, **Fig 7.3**, the photo shows a wooden framed and glass case which I made for a steam yacht. Glass in the four sides and top makes it quite a long job and you may feel that something simpler would suffice.

A very easy project is to make a box and only put glass in the side facing you. The case is usually painted white inside. A small light inside will illuminate the model but ventilation will need to be allowed for. Use an everlasting bulb – these burn cool. Those who are artists as well as modelmakers can try their hand at a seascape on the back wall of the case. This is very effective with small waterline models. If these can be made and placed in a shallow case they can be hung like a picture.

Ordinary model ship mounts can be divided into cradle mounts and column mounts. The cradle mount is usually cut out and follows the cross-section shape of the hull, a quarter the length in from both ends. These 'U' pieces are fixed at right-angles on the mount base and can be lined with leather or baize.

The column mount will give you a wide choice of styles. Turned brass ones give a model class while a turned wooden column in ebony yew or birdseye walnut can also look very attractive. Plain brass rods both solid and hollow are quite suitable. The odd cartridge case in brass can save you money.

Most models have a keel blade and any column used will have to have a dip filed or cut in the top for the keel blade to rest in. Some models will need other supporting rods to stop the hull wobbling. One pair of these placed each side of the hull amidships is usually sufficient to stop any tendency to wobble. One last point: always make sure that the model's waterline is parallel with the mount base. The drawings of different mounts will give you an idea of the way you can make these. See **Fig 10.13**.

Materials for model building

Wood

Throughout the various chapters I have mentioned some of the materials you will need for building from scratch. Here are two more.

I suppose the type of wood you use is more important to the modeller making a solid hull than those making a plank on frame one. How hard or soft the wood is can make quite a difference to the finish. Another factor to consider is the straightness of grain and the absence of knots in your wood.

I like shaping solid hulls from conifer types of wood. Ordinary pine and cedar wood seem sympathetic to my efforts as long as I select the pieces I use. If you have not done any shaping from the solid you may like to try a lump of balsa wood. This comes in various weights but some are too soft so choose a harder type – it will still be softer than a block of pine. Large pieces can be expensive so make up a block from two or three pieces, checking they are all of the same degree of hardness.

The model built with planks on bulkhead frames can be made with plywood for the frames and lime or other types of wood for the planks, like obeche.

The ply is usually ⅛in. thick. On larger models you can use thicker plywood in the centre sections where edge shaping is not needed. Try to use good quality birch ply as it seems to be more rigid and better made than some Far Eastern plywood.

Deck laying is usually made with the lighter coloured plank. It is best to lay a deck onto a solid base like a sheet of ¹⁄₁₆in. or ¹⁄₃₂in. ply glued over the bulkheads. If you lay a deck directly onto the tops of the various bulkheads you will need a thicker plank to avoid a wavy or dipping deck surface.

Those with limited time for hobbies might like to try sheets of printed or already scored planks. These can be bought from model shops.

Metal

Copper and brass are mostly used in modelmaking.

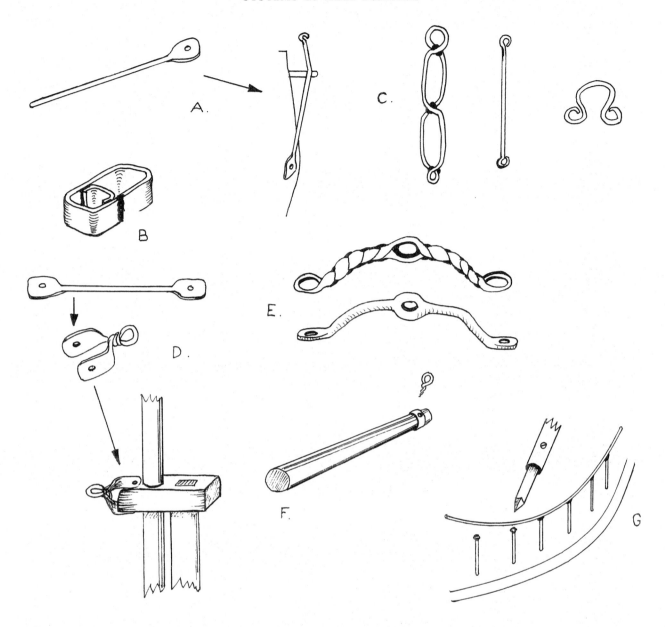

*Fig 10.14 A The thicker type of electric wire cable, made of copper, can be used for making the rod type of chainplates. **B** Sheet metal strip can be made into a convincing mast cap with the help of a little soldering. **C** Wire, when twisted and soldered on the crossovers, will make old-style chainplates. **D** Wire, beaten each end and drilled can make an iron crane fitting after twisting. Use a flathead punch with hammer if a small flat is wanted. **E** Thick copper wire can be twisted and coated with solder to make an iron swivel truss. The thicker variety of wire when beaten in the middle and ends can also make a swivel truss after bending. **F** Wire, when looped and twisted tight, can make small ring irons. Sharpen with a file and drill yards etc. before gluing in. **G** In the more modern ship you can knock brass flathead nails into the deck and top off with a rail made of wire soldered to the head tops.*

Soft iron wire in about two gauges is useful. If the non-ferrous metal is too rigid you can soften it by annealing (heat up with gas torch to cherry red then quench in water). In some areas on your model you assimilate iron banding of timbers etc. with strips of brown paper tape. This is the old-fashioned glued tape used for parcels before the age of Sellotape! With a ruler cut off strips the width required then dampen and roll around to the thickness required. Paint black to finish after the gum strip is thoroughly dry. A pair of round-nosed pliers, the jeweller's small type, is most useful when using thin strips and metal wire so keep them handy, together with a pair of small tin snips or old scissors.

Many of the models we make are pre-1800. In those days very little metal was used on the yards and various spars. Much was accomplished by using ropes to loop and truss before patent methods using iron yard and mast bands came about.

As mentioned above, soft iron wire is a useful item to have in your workbox. Various thin-walled brass and copper tube is another. I always save old radio aerials – after a good rubbing with emery cloth they make excellent metal bands.

After the 1800s rope slings and trusses gave way to metal (see Chapter 11 **Fig 11.7B**). We can make these from wire if twisted the right way and supported with solder, sheet copper is also useful.

Chainplates, the strap type, can be made from sheet metal suitably cut with snips, or wire of a thick variety if the rod type of chainplate is made.

A good soldering iron, a small steel block to act as an anvil, a good medium to small ball-pein hammer and small-round nosed pliers are all you need. See **Fig 10.14**.

11 Rigging your models and sail making

Rigging a model ship is one job that demands patience and perseverance. It's a fiddly job which on some models takes many days and sometimes months – the larger the model the longer the job. In smaller models, around twelve to fourteen inches long, everything is so small that minor details are often left out as being too small to handle.

It is very important to get the order of rigging correct otherwise you will find yourself doing a bit of keyhole surgery which shouldn't really be necessary. Most enthusiasts know the difference between standing and running rigging. It is the standing rigging, like mast main braces that come first, followed usually by lower shrouds.

I ought to mention at this stage the method used on large models. You set the mast as if you were building the real thing. For example, the main lower mast is set in place followed by the tops or crosstrees. In this case the shrouds come first, these being looped over the mast before fitting the next section of mast and mast cap. If this is done there would obviously be no upper attachment points for the fixing of main brace on the upper masts.

In most cases we make up our masts in their entirety before mounting into the hull including tops and crosstrees etc. If you are wise, you will fix any pulleys and other purchase points to the mast sections before mounting. In particular, the pulleys used to lift yard arms, mizzen and gaff poles. The making of a 3rd Rater in Chapter 2 is a good example showing the order of things.

Once you have the main braces in place followed by the lower shrouds, the jobs more or less dictate themselves.

For instance, when all the yards on a square-rigged vessel are made, look at your plan carefully. All blocks that are attached to yards, and in the case of fore and aft sailing boats the gaff poles and booms, need the blocks attaching to the yards and other spars before fixing to the masts – see **Fig 11.2**, top drawing. This will save a lot of frustration later on.

The yards are hung onto the masts in a number of different ways. The lower yards are much heavier than those found at the top of masts. This is reflected in the strength of the attachment method and block sizes. See **Figs 11.5** and **11.6**. Different periods of ships had different methods of attachment. Rope slings were superseded by patent metal crane swivels and iron swivel trusses. See **Fig 11.8 M** and **Q** and **Fig 11.7B**. Your plan might show these details – if not you will have to do some research. On large naval ships the main course yard had additional safeguards like heavy chains to reinforce this vulnerable area in battle.

Belaying pin rails should be glued and pinned or nailed onto the inside bulwarks early on. Drill these first before fitting, their position in relation to the masts will be indicated on the plan.

I am always being asked about the kind of tension that should be shown in running rigging i.e. should it loop slack or be taut? My answer is some and some. One of the difficulties is finding a rigging thread that will hang slack without wrinkles. Waxing with a candle sometimes straightens cordage, or a little hot water in a cup with a hank of cord well soaked then put under tension to dry may solve the problem.

Yard braces (used to swing the yard) can be shown with a slight bow of slackness, but most of the rest should be shown fairly tight. Look at your rigging plan.

The termination of all running rigging at deck level should finish as a well-flaked coil on the belaying pin rail or fife rail (at the butt of the masts). This is sometimes difficult to do in situ, so I suggest you tie off the descending cordage and cut off any over after attaching to rail or belaying pin. Take a length of cordage and wind a separate coil (away from the model) using a little matt colourless glue. When this is dry and shaped correctly just attach it to the belaying point on the model – if you can do this without the glue all the better. It will look authentic and will have saved you a lot of fiddling.

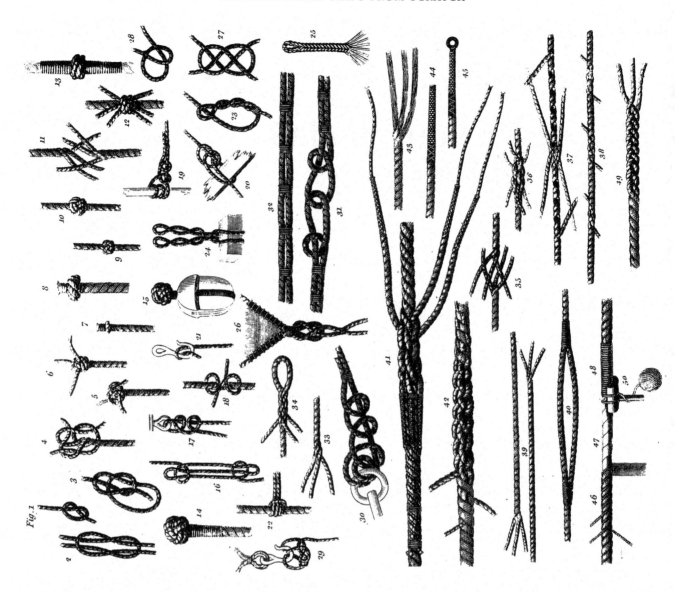

Fig 11.1 (above) and 11.2 (right) *These reproductions on 'rigging' come from my collection of old engravings. I have a few pages only from the original book, published by Longhamn, Hurst, Rees, Orme & Brown 1st October 1816. The engravings first appeared in 1794 in* Elements and Practice of Rigging *by David Steel, re-published in 1818 as* The Art of Rigging. *In 1974 Fisher Nautical Press, Brighton, reprinted Steel's* Art of Rigging 1818 *from an original copy of the book. This is a useful addition to the modelmaker's library.*

The threading of blocks can be really frustrating as most blocks that you buy need opening up a little. I have a very fine drill permanently fixed in a pin vice for this job. Burning through with a red hot needle can be used if you do it quickly. If you make your own blocks and deadeyes you can make sure the holes are big enough to start with. Any strands of rigging that prove difficult to thread can have the tips dipped in a little fast-setting glue and squeezed into a sharp point before they are dry. This need for tapering and whipping cordage ends was used on period ships. See **Fig 11.1**.

The pulley blocks that need to be attached to the masts, yards and cordage in running rigging and haul ropes need a loop of some sort. In some instances, soft iron florists' wire is used around the block where attachment to a deck ring or mast

section is needed. Those lines, for instance, that drop from yard tips for the yard braces are directly attached to the blocks. Whatever way you find best for you is really the way to approach this job, as long as it looks authentic.

The hobby shops dealing in model ships usually have a good selection of cordage of different types. If you want to make your own, twisting various numbers of thinner lines together using a hand drill with a cup hook in the chuck can be quite successful, providing you keep the length under tension. Rub a pad soaked in a little PVA glue along its length and keep taut until dry. This method is very useful when trying to find the correct gauge for main braces on the larger model ships. Staining the rigging before use should have been done for all standing rigging. Black shoe dye is usually matt black or eggshell

RIGGING.

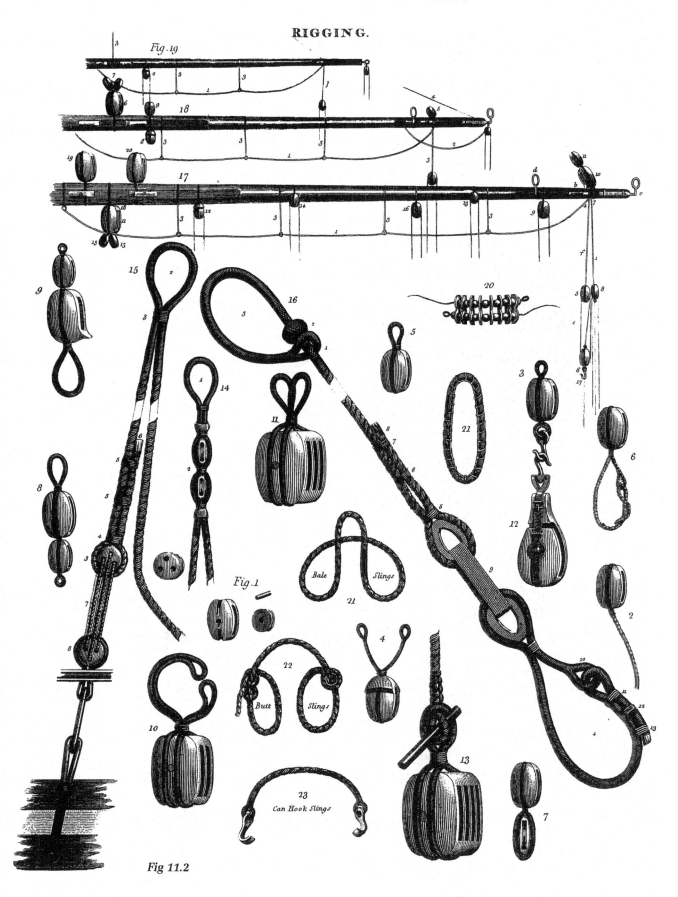

Fig 11.2

when dry. Do this messy job well away from the model! Other running rigging comes in various shades of beige, fawn or off-white. Tea or coffee will dye these lighter lines a shade darker if required.

A little gauge tool is useful when lacing together the deadeye of shrouds to the chainplate deadeyes with the lanyard cord. It ensures that the space is constant between deadeyes, holding these at the

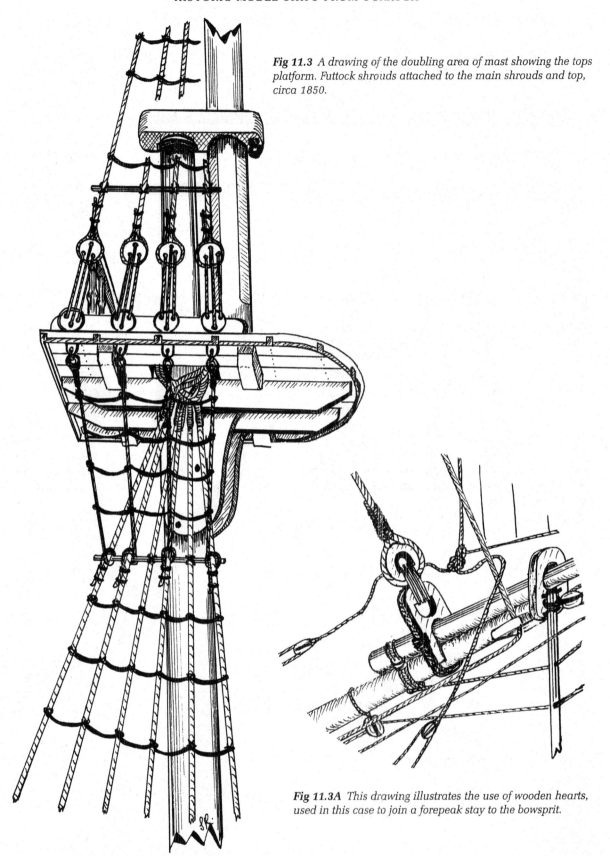

Fig 11.3 *A drawing of the doubling area of mast showing the tops platform. Futtock shrouds attached to the main shrouds and top, circa 1850.*

Fig 11.3A *This drawing illustrates the use of wooden hearts, used in this case to join a forepeak stay to the bowsprit.*

correct distance until the threading is tight enough and non-slippery enough for you to remove the gauge. After many years of modelmaking I have disposed of this gauge but it is useful for beginners. (See Chapter 9, **Fig 9.18**.)

Heat and humidity can affect your rigging. Over-

taut rigging can distort yard arms and mizzen booms if too tight to start with – this is a minor possibility but worth a mention.

Deadeyes

These can be made as described in *Model Ships from*

Scratch. Like blocks, you will need many of these and hobby shops can supply them in different woods and qualities. I would not advise the use of plastic deadeyes – you have to paint them a darker colour and this is inclined to block up the holes whereas wood can be stained with thin spirit dyes and avoids this problem.

Maritime Models of Greenwich and *Euro Models of Twickenham* can supply very good deadeyes and I have to admit that of late I have started using these. Laziness has reared its ugly head. My last model used up two hundred deadeyes and to have made them would not have improved my fingertips!

Before the use of the three-hole deadeyes, ships used a form of heart. An oval or triangular wood block, grooved for rope or lanyard with a large centre hold. See **Fig 11.3A**. This provided a degree of purchase when setting the stays or shrouds up taut. Steel's *Art of Rigging 1818* and R. C. Anderson's *Seventeenth Century Rigging* are two very useful books if you are a serious modelmaker (see Bibliography).

Try to remember that it doesn't matter how good the hull and deck detail is – if the rigging is rotten you have a failure on your hands.

Ratlines

This part of the chapter should be subtitled 'Frustration' for some of us. As I have found, a massive amount of patience is needed combined with the manual dexterity of a brain surgeon – this is usually a long task for which there are no short cuts.

I well remember seeing my children, with a plastic kit, simply cutting out the piece of netting supplied to a conical shape and sticking it onto the mast – that was the shrouds and ratlines finished, about five minutes flat.

To do this job properly you really do have to tie each ratline with at least the kind of knot known as an overhand or thumb knot. Some ratline cord will be quite secure even on the outside shrouds tied like this. If you find the cord you have tends to be a little springy, like some synthetics, then you will need a double thumb knot on the two outside shrouds. The centre shrouds, be they one, two or more, can have a single knot. See **Fig 11.4**.

The shrouds, being standing rigging, are usually of a thicker grade of cord and dark in colour. The foot ropes or ratlines need to be of a light cord as they were in reality. The slight contrast looks good on the finished rigging.

Sometimes, perhaps a few days after finishing the ratlines, you will see one or two of the outside shroud knots undoing themselves. A temperature change can cause this. To avoid this happening, put a dab of white glue on these outside knots – it will dry clear and stop any knots coming loose.

Tension is something you have to deal with on the shrouds and ratlines – as well as your own! If your shroud lines are nice and tight and you don't treat them too roughly when tying the ratlines across, then you will have no trouble. It is like knitting: a constant and equal tension is required throughout the operation if you want to avoid a set of shrouds that look like the Eiffel Tower! See **Fig 11.4A**.

One thing that will help to avoid this happening is the tying on of sheer poles. These were usually positioned above the deadeyes making the first step up the shrouds. Being stiff, this sheer pole keeps the line of shrouds evenly spaced. You can put another sheer pole halfway up your lines – this was done on the larger ships and you will find it most useful in stopping a horrible bowing in the lines as mentioned above.

When you get near to the tops or the mast doubling area where the shrouds finish, the shroud lines are very close together. Try to tie off every ratline, even though it becomes very fiddly.

The 3rd Rater model in Chapter 2 had eleven shrouds on each side of the fore and main mast and ten on either side of the mizzen – a total of sixty-four shrouds, not to mention all the other stay lines descending to deck level. I did not dare count the number of individual knots tied when ratlining this model.

The end result is what keeps you going on jobs like this. It is important to give yourself a break every so often and do another job on the model. Alternatively have a coffee – or something stronger!

A note on ships' masts

In early times masts were made from a single spar of wood such as a whole trunk of a pine tree. As sailing ships developed in the 17th and 18th centuries, it became necessary to increase the number of sails and therefore upper masts. The single trunk masts were not strong enough to carry the additional upper weight and wind effect. The circumference of the lower mast needed to be increased and trees of this new thickness were in short supply, so lower masts were made up from a number of vertical timbers and joined together with wooden pegs, iron bands and some unique types of joinery. Additional strengthening pieces were also fixed vertically to naval ships. See Chapter 2, 3rd Rater masts. Upper masts were still made from single pieces. See **Fig 11.6A**.

Single topsails and double topsails

Before the 1800s the topsail was attached to the topsail yard. See **Fig 11.7**. It was a large sail and needed a large crew to work it efficiently.

As the 1850s approached, a new system was needed to enable a reduction in crew numbers to manage top sails so the double topsail was intro-

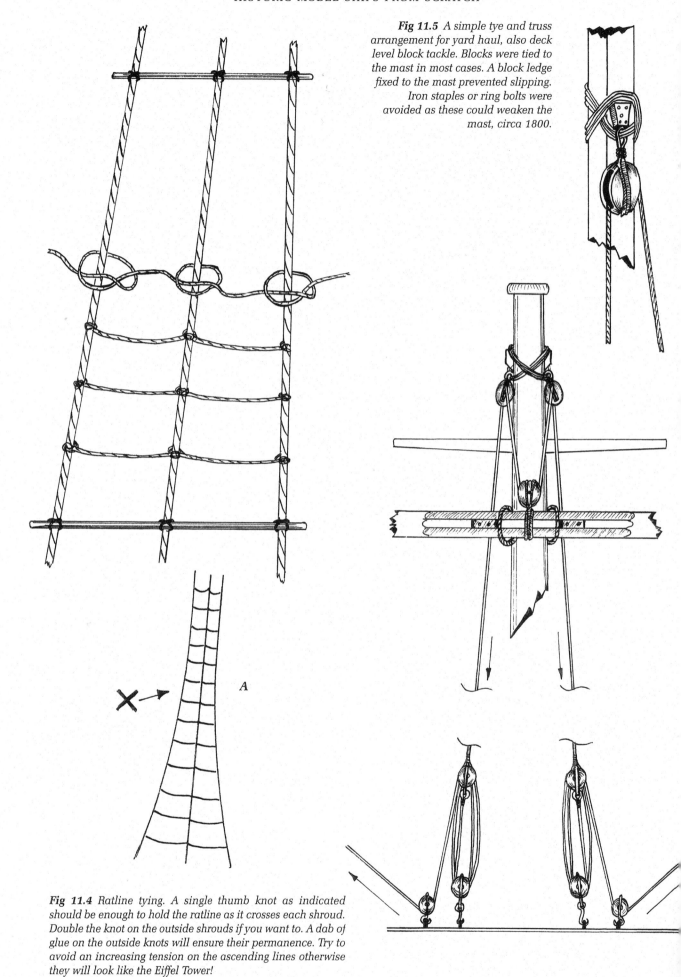

Fig 11.5 *A simple tye and truss arrangement for yard haul, also deck level block tackle. Blocks were tied to the mast in most cases. A block ledge fixed to the mast prevented slipping. Iron staples or ring bolts were avoided as these could weaken the mast, circa 1800.*

A

Fig 11.4 *Ratline tying. A single thumb knot as indicated should be enough to hold the ratline as it crosses each shroud. Double the knot on the outside shrouds if you want to. A dab of glue on the outside knots will ensure their permanence. Try to avoid an increasing tension on the ascending lines otherwise they will look like the Eiffel Tower!*

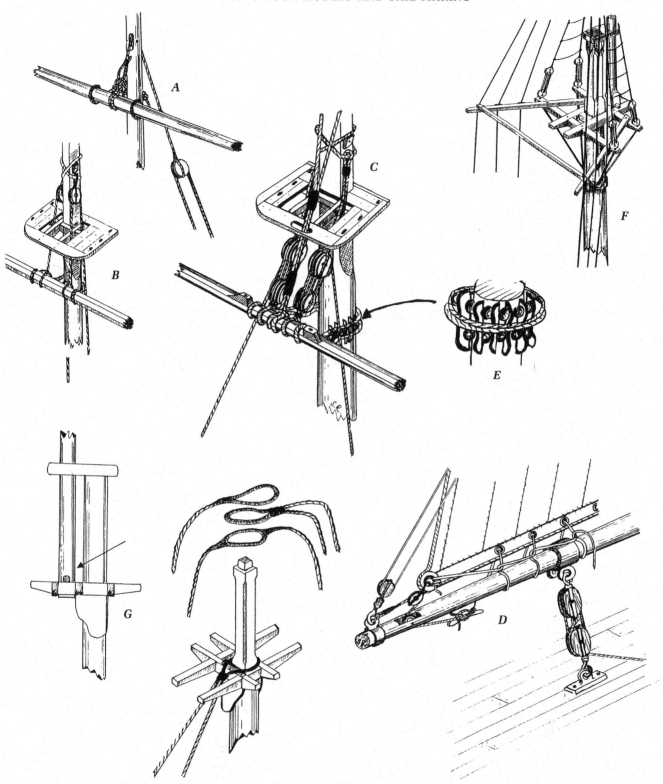

Fig 11.6 A *Topgallant yard with simple single haul halliard. A rope parral truss is bent on the yard to keep it in place.* **B** *Lower mast with simple tackle, double haul halliard, a rope parral in place.* **C** *Heavy tackle with yard on two pairs of triple purchase blocks (jeers). A rope parral truss and a safety sling to lower mast cap is fitted.* **D** *A spanker mizzen boom, showing the method of lacing foot of sail with lanyard to the boom (Fisherman's bend).* **E** *A parral made up of ribs, the vertical separators, and the trucks, the wooden balls alternately threaded between the ribs. This helped the yard to move smoothly up and down and swivel around the mast when bracing sail. A model would have to be of a large scale to show this detail.* **F** *A topgallant mast of the 1850s onwards. Spreaders bolted across the frame of the crosstrees at an angle diverging towards the mast held out the backstay support rigging on the spreader bar with cleats. This gave better support to the topgallant mast. Futtock irons are fitted from the iron mast collar giving added strength to the crosstree frame.* **G** *Here the shroud rigging can be looped over the lower mast in a number of ways providing you are not pre-assembling your masts. This would prevent you looping over the shrouds because the mast cap would be fixed. Always plan for a reasonable space at the doubling of the mast to accommodate the shroud ropes – see arrow. On smaller ships where you have pre-assembled the mast, shrouds can simply be threaded up and over the mast head from one side to the other once the mast is set permanently in the deck.*

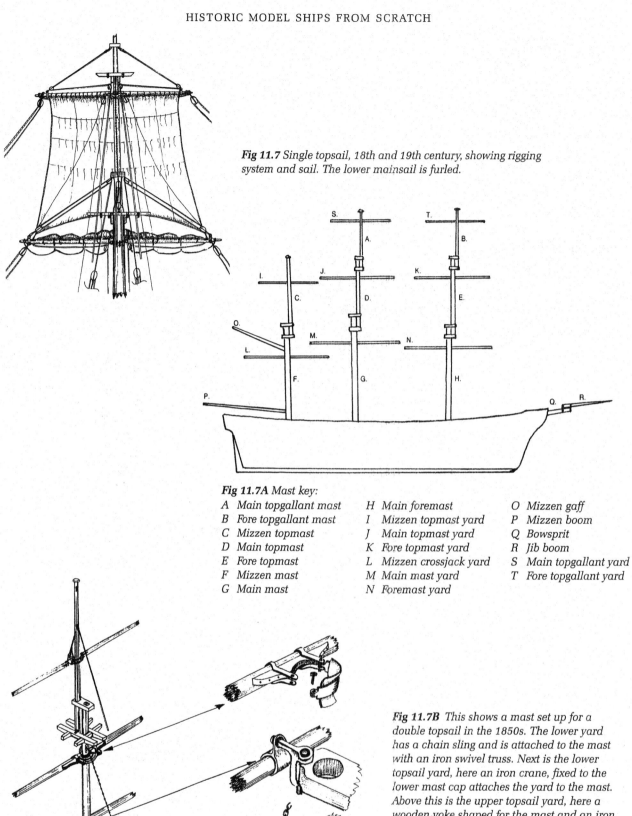

Fig 11.7 *Single topsail, 18th and 19th century, showing rigging system and sail. The lower mainsail is furled.*

Fig 11.7A *Mast key:*

A Main topgallant mast
B Fore topgallant mast
C Mizzen topmast
D Main topmast
E Fore topmast
F Mizzen mast
G Main mast

H Main foremast
I Mizzen topmast yard
J Main topmast yard
K Fore topmast yard
L Mizzen crossjack yard
M Main mast yard
N Foremast yard

O Mizzen gaff
P Mizzen boom
Q Bowsprit
R Jib boom
S Main topgallant yard
T Fore topgallant yard

Fig 11.7B *This shows a mast set up for a double topsail in the 1850s. The lower yard has a chain sling and is attached to the mast with an iron swivel truss. Next is the lower topsail yard, here an iron crane, fixed to the lower mast cap attaches the yard to the mast. Above this is the upper topsail yard, here a wooden yoke shaped for the mast and an iron liner held the yard to the mast. The topgallant yard was held with a similar yoke and parral, the halliard sheaved at the mast head.*

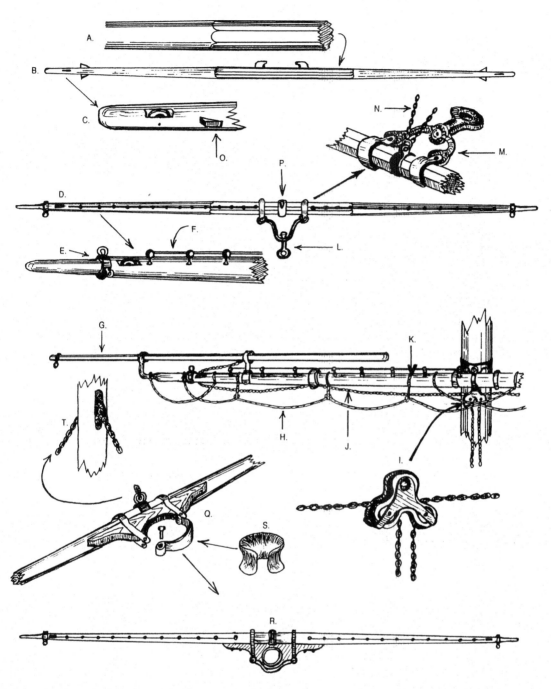

Fig 11.8

A Yard centre, eight-sided
B Lower yard – before 1800s
C Yard end – sheave and cleat
D Lower yard – before 1850s
E Yard end, band and sheave
F Jackstay bar
G Studding sail boom

H Foot rope
I Double sheet block
J Chain sheet to boom
K Stirrup rope to footrope
L Iron swivel – 1850s
M Detail of iron truss swivel 1850s
N Chain sling to mast

0 Wooden cleats for sail ring
P Band for chain sling
Q Yard yoke and tub parral
R Topsail yard – 1850s
S Iron liner for tub parral
T Chain sling to mast sheave at mast-
head

Note: G, H, I, J & K shows a 19th-century yard. Earlier types were less sophisticated.

duced. This virtually made two sails from the old larger topsail, each with its own yard. These new sails could be managed quicker when it was necessary to reduce sail areas when bad weather struck. The main course yard (the lowest sail) was attached in much the same way as before. The new lower top sail yard was attached to the lower mast cap with an iron crane. The upper topsail yard was held to the mast by a wooden yoke fixed to the yard and shaped to fit around the side of the mast. A movable tub parral lined with a thick iron liner and well greased held everything together. See **Fig 11.7B**.

Obviously you would only show the above detail of fixing yards to masts on the larger models, and even then a few short cuts may be necessary! Simple rope parrals can be used on the smaller type of model.

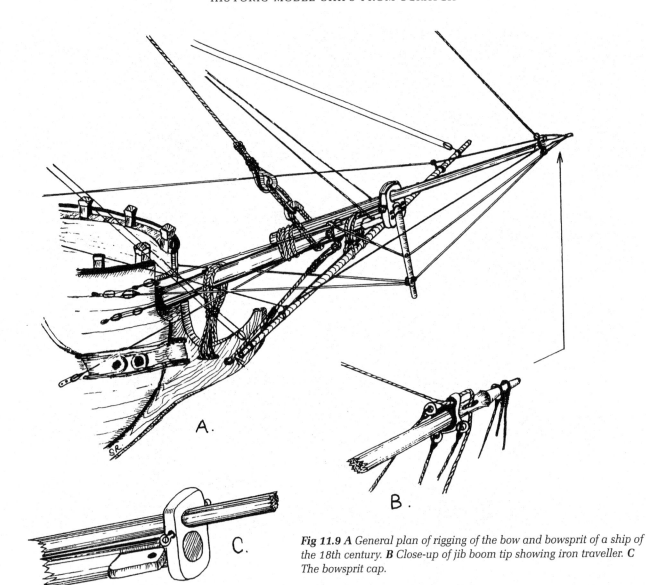

A.

B.

C.

Fig 11.9 A *General plan of rigging of the bow and bowsprit of a ship of the 18th century.* **B** *Close-up of jib boom tip showing iron traveller.* **C** *The bowsprit cap.*

Lacing sails to yards

Before 1800 sails were laced to yards with robbands or rope-bands through eyelets at the head of each square sail and wound around the yard. Early in the 1800s jackstays were introduced. This rope ran along the top side of the yard held in place with eye bolts, later replaced by an iron bar. See **Fig 11.8 E** and **F**. The sail robbands were laced around these and through the eyelets as in modern ships. Again this detail would only be shown if your model is large enough for it to be visible, otherwise a simple lacing around the yard is sufficient for the smaller model.

Fitting sails to a model

To finish a model with rigging only and no sails is a fairly common practice and is probably best if the model is to remain uncased. If sails are fitted then a case is a good idea as models do get very dusty and nobody goes near them with a duster for fear of damaging the rigging etc.

If we make sails it is a question of choosing material with the weave in scale and the flexibility to work with easily. Forget trying to shape with gore cuts (cut on the cross) to get a balloon effect on square riggers – just cut them out leaving enough around the edges to turn over into a seam edge.

Some plans will indicate the run of the weave. Bolts of canvas were of a fairly constant width so it was necessary to join these lengths together to make up the whole sail area. See **Fig 11.11**.

When making sails for a completed model it is best to first cut paper templates. Most sail plans are not in scale with the rest of the ship's plan which makes it difficult for a beginner unless the sail plan can be enlarged. Over the years of modelmaking I have found it easier to let the finished model dictate the exact sizes of sail, using the sail plan as an aid only.

I pin sheets of thin typing paper to boom, yards and head bracings with pegs or clips and carefully pencil the exact size. Allowing for bowing of square

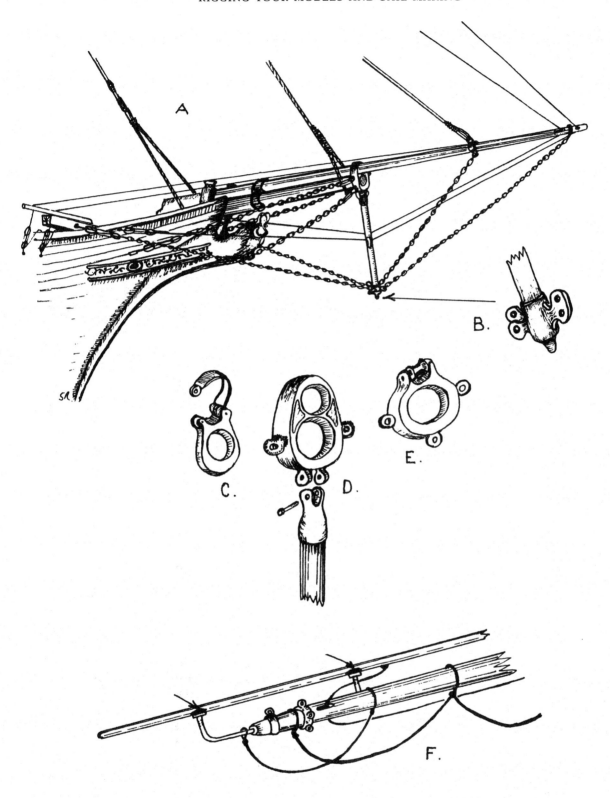

Fig 11.10 A *A general plan of rigging of the bow and bowsprit section of a ship, circa 1850 onwards.* **B** *Martingale tip iron.* **C** *Saddle collar iron.* **D** *Bowsprit cap incorporating martingale cap connector.* **E** *Bowsprit boom collar to connect chain to martingale and forming other rigging connection points.* **F** *Close-up of stuntsail boom and fittings when making a model. Two small flathead nails are fixed into the yard and glued. One is bent at right-angles. The stuntsail boom is then glued to the heads of each nail (see arrow points).*

sail, cut the paper exactly to the finished size of sails. Place these templates onto the material. Allow for turning and seaming (about ¼in. to ⅛in.) by using a ruler and drawing a line with a soft pencil parallel with the template edge but away from it. When this is finished, the cut-out sails should be pressed with a warm iron. Fold over the edges while pressing as it makes it easier to machine these

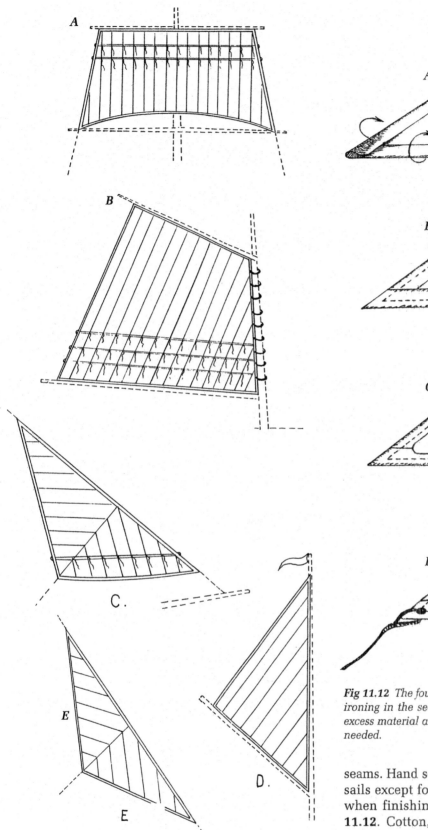

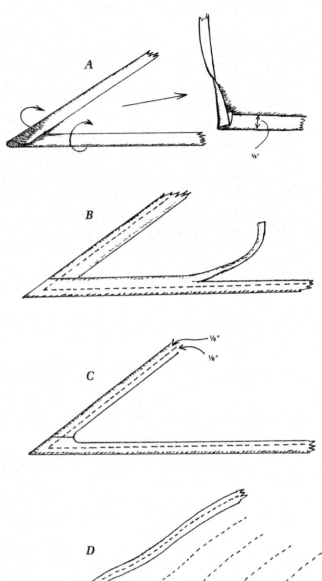

Fig 11.12 The four stages of sail making consist of cutting out, ironing in the seam turn and sewing. To finish, cut off any excess material along seam edge. You can then press again if needed.

seams. Hand sewing isn't a good idea when making sails except for the corners and sheet attachments when finishing off. See the various stages at **Fig 11.12**. Cotton, cotton and polyester, thin calico, unbleached -- are all useful materials to make sails from. Try to get cream, beige or light fawn coloured material. It may be necessary to do your own dyeing but be warned about dyeing *after* completing the sails – you can start with sails fit for a 3rd Rater and end up with a set that will fit a frigate!

Fig 11.11 Five types of sails. **A** A square sail. **B** A mizzen sail often called a spanker on square-rigged ships. This can be a mainsail on a cutter. **C** A jib sail. These head sails can be of different sizes on the same ship, i.e. a flying jib etc. **D** Mizzen topsail or a cutter's topsail. **E** Staysail, often rigged between fore topmast and main topmast. On some motor-driven craft a mizzen staysail is the only sail. Mostly used on fishing boats when fishing stationary to keep the head to wind.

12 Christopher Columbus and Sir Francis Drake – the ships they sailed in

On August 3rd 1492, Columbus set sail on what he called his 'Enterprise of the Indies'. His flagship was the *Santa Maria*, a Galician nao (ship) with a northern Spanish crew. It is a story we all learnt about at school. The two other ships were caravels, a relatively small Mediterranean trading vessel. The *Nina* was rigged as a conventional ship, like the *Santa Maria* and the *Pinta* was lateen rigged. Both of these

Fig 12.2 *Close-up of* Nina *deck and poop, showing chainplates and two small rail-mounted cannons.*

were smaller than the *Santa Maria* (95ft long) at 56ft and 58ft overall respectively.

When the *Nina* set sail she was a caravela latina, but the Atlantic weather proved difficult and in the Canary Islands her rig was changed to what was called caravela rotunda.

After making it to the Indies Columbus returned to Europe in the *Nina*, leaving the *Santa Maria* as living quarters for those left behind, later to perish at the hand of local Indians.

Nina is shown here as the model I made from excellent details and information found in the *National Geographic* magazine. Although she was featured in my last book, I show different pictures here. As for the *Santa Maria*, there have been so many models of this ship, all different, that nobody can say for certain exactly what she looked like. Some years ago a full-size reconstruction could be seen in the harbour at Barcelona. Being the largest of the three ships I am sure she had a fairly substantial built-up forecastle.

The small drawing **Fig 12.5** tries to show the relative differences in the three ships. These little ships

Fig 12.1 *The finished* Nina *on mahogany stand.*

Fig 12.3 Another view of Nina. *A brass plate attached to the stand gives her date and name.*

Fig 12.4 A stern view showing type of rudder and poop overhang.

Fig 12.5 My drawing of the three ships of Columbus' fleet with a certain amount of artist's licence – Santa Maria, Nina *and* Pinta.

make handsome models giving you the opportunity of a very colourful painting job.

The *Golden Hind*

This is the ship in which, from 1577 to 1580, Francis Drake circumnavigated the globe. Originally named the *Pelican*, Drake changed the name to *Golden Hind* when he reached the Magellan Straits in honour of his patron, Sir Christopher Hatton, whose family crest was a hind. *Golden Hind* was the only ship of the five vessels that set sail to make it back to Plymouth, dropping anchor in Plymouth Sound on 26th September 1580. Drake brought home quite a lot of treasure and the *Golden Hind* became famous.

106

Fig 12.6A Golden Hind *at the Brighton Marina during a visit in 1996.* **B** *The jib boom with the spritsail boom crossing it. Note the hearts used for lashing and tensioning the main brace on foremast (not in picture).* **C** *Stern view of* Golden Hind *showing the hind crest.* **D & F** *The forecastle and port shrouds of foremast.* **E** *Bow and figurehead of the* Golden Hind. *See the gammoning rope at the base of the bowsprit.*

Fig 12.6 Golden Hind *at the Brighton Marina.* **G** *The main top, in this case it could be called a crow's nest.* **H** *As above.* **I** *The various main yards with furled sails.* **J** *The mizzen mast showing crosstrees and wooden mast cap holding top mast. (Ignore the radar aerials!)*

She was docked in a special dock at Deptford where the public were admitted to view her on payment of a small sum, the money going to charities (nothing changes!).

Another *Golden Hind* sailed with Sir Humphrey Gilbert in 1583 to form a colony in Newfoundland.

The reason that I have included this ship is that there is a very good modern reproduction of this

vessel. It visited Brighton in 1996 and the interesting picture here reproduced shows in detail what she was like for those who might like to try a model. Nexus Plans Service No. SY2 is a plan by Stanley Rogers. It is 18in. long. The pictures will help with the finer detail – you can leave out the modern navigational aerials!

The modern reproduction seems to be faithful to

Fig 12.7 Nina, *the second ship in Columbus' fleet, is thought to have carried ten early breech-loading swivel guns called bombardas. This drawing shows one of these with breech in position and held in by a wedge which was hammered into position.*

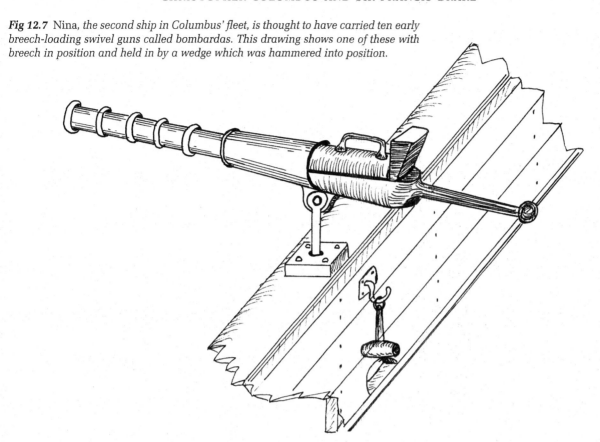

the designs of the period with the exception, for safety's sake, of a few items.

Making *Nina*

Because of the hull's full figure and the lack of a proper plan, I made the lower part of the hull solid. It was carved and finished in the usual way. The poop deck area and bulwarks were built up from model planking. I have used hearts for shroud ends and not deadeyes. The details in the *National Geo-*

graphic magazine seemed fairly certain on this point.

As for the number of masts, I gave *Nina* an extra small lateen sail. The detail I worked from showed this although many illustrations I have seen do not have one.

It is a nice model to make and with no real plans a lot of fun can be had going through books and other sources of research.

I intend to make the *Golden Hind* in the near future, using the plan mentioned but with the helpful detailed photographs shown here.

13 Old ships make interesting models

The history of the ship and the boat is like looking at one long ongoing experiment by those involved in their development.

As a modelmaker, one cannot help being interested in the development of floating craft. The numbers are so vast that we should never run out of models to make. These numbers can be divided into boats and ships, enlarging still further the choice we have.

A boat is usually a small open craft without any decking and usually oar driven. Some exceptions to this definition are fishing boats which sometimes have half decks and sails. Submarines are generally known as boats. A ship (old English, scip) in maritime terms is a vessel with three masts, bowsprit and square rigged – usually referred to as 'she'!

A good look at all the types available to make as models won't be wasted. There is something here to suit the tastes of every modelmaker.

Types of sailing craft 1600BC to AD1900

Egyptian galley 1600BC
Single mast and square sail, 30 oarsmen.

Assyrian galley 700BC
Single mast, single square-rigged sail, 40 or more oarsmen.

Phoenician traders 600BC
Single mast, square rigged.

Greek triremes 400BC
An important war boat, 30 to 40 oarsmen. Single mast, square sail.

Roman war galley 150BC
Single mast, large square sail. 50 or more oarsmen.

Drakar (Danish longship) AD780
This type of longship raided the southern coast of Wessex in 787. Similar raids continued for over a hundred years ending when Canute became King of England.

Viking longship
A very similar sailing boat with square sails on a mast that could be lowered with about 24 oarsmen. Some were very large – 120ft – with 64 oarsmen. The Viking ships cover a long period of history. In England and other parts of northern Europe, the longboat developed into a wider and deeper hulled vessel, allowing for larger sails with less reliance on oar power.

Ship of the Cinque Ports 1200
Our knowledge of this type comes entirely from contemporary seals – Sandwich, Dover and Winchelsea all had moulded images of ships on them. It is difficult to be certain of the real shape of these vessels given the small space on the seals. We know they were clincher- or clinker-built with deep sheer and high stemposts and sternposts carrying forecastles and stern castles. See **Fig 13.5A**.

Crusader ship 1250
Bluff bow and stern craft, lateen rigged with two masts. This was a Mediterranean ship built mostly in Venice.

English ship 1426
John, Duke of Bedford, Lord High Admiral of England had on his official seal a fine example of an English ship of the mid-1400s. A vessel approximately 60ft long, again clincher-built with a rudder mounted on sternpost. The bow was sharper than the stern. The forecastle was a fighting platform but the after-castle was extended to provide covered accommodation. See **Fig 13.5B**.

Fig 13.1 *A second model of* My Lady, *a topsail schooner, on brass columns mounted on mahogany plinth. This one is fully rigged.*

Fig 13.2 *The author with model of* My Lady, *a topsail schooner. Note: there were plenty of these small schooners around from 1860 onwards. Those that survived ended up being used by enthusiastic weekend sailors in the 1920s. The Nexus Plans Service has a couple of plans – namely No. SY32 a TS schooner with rigging and sail plan, also No. MM 909 (30in. long) by L. R. Armstrong. This latter is a sandwich-formed hull.*

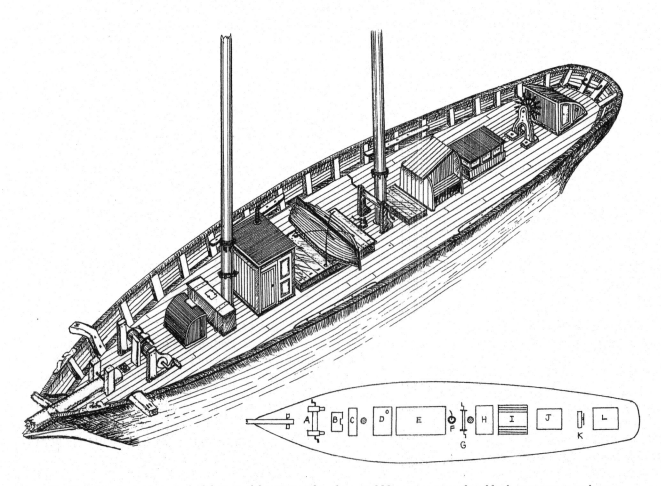

Fig 13.3 *A typical schooner deck layout of the 1890s. This ship would have accommodated both passengers and cargo.*

The carrack 1480

This vessel was a transformation in design from single to three masts. The Flemish carrack circa 1450 was carvel-built, giving a much stronger hull than the clincher-built ships. This was necessary due to the increase in ordnance weights that were now developing. There were also many Mediterranean versions of the carrack.

English cog 1485

There are drawings of ships in the manuscript entitled *The Pageant of Richard Beauchamp, Earl of Warwick* in the British Museum. The date of these drawings and descriptions is thought to be between 1485 and 1490. These are probably the most accurate images of English ships of this period.

These were clincher-built with a triangular forecastle, projecting well over the stem not unlike the earlier English ship of the 1420s.

Spanish caravel 1492

The *Santa Maria* is a good example of this type of vessel. Three masts, the fore and main masts with square-rigged sails, with the mizzen as a lateen rig. Carvel built.

The Portuguese caravela 1530

In the Mediterranean various craft were developing to suit the sea conditions of that area. Other craft suitable for longer and more arduous trips into other oceans were being built. A Portuguese caravela used by Emperor Charles V to capture Tunis in 1535 was lateen rigged on three masts with another mast high on the forecastle wearing a square sail. This ship was over a hundred feet long with a thirty foot beam.

This combination of rig lasted well beyond the end of the century and similar rigged vessels were known variously as Mediterranean barks, polacres or xebecs.

Fig 13.4 *This reproduction from old engravings comes from the section on 'vessels' in the* Royal Encyclopaedia *1791, like other originals shown in the chapter on 3rd Raters. The eleven ships illustrated show the variety of different craft used in the 1700s and early 1800s. From the top, left to right: ketch; galley; snow; dogger; brig; sloop; schooner; bilander; galliot; 3rd Rater; xebec. They are included for your interest. They may help to start you off into further research and a new model to make.*

Fig 13.5A *A ship of 1284 from the seal of Dover. More symbolic than strictly accurate.*

Fig 13.5B *An English ship of the latter half of the 15th century. A reasonably accurate picture.*

Elizabethan galleon 1600

In the Pepysian Library at Magdalene College, Cambridge, is a set of plans, the earliest known in England. These were made by Matthew Baker about 1586. He was a master shipwright and his plans show the exact form of Elizabethan ships. The four-mast rig was normal for large men-of-war. The Science Museum model of the *Elizabeth Jonas* is a combination of the Matthew Baker plans mentioned above. She was square-rigged on foremast and mainmast, lateen-rigged on the third and mizzen-mast. Her keel length was one hundred feet, her beam thirty eight feet, with a good depth of hold, eighteen feet.

Herring buss 1600–1700

North Sea fishing was carried out by large sturdy vessels known as busses. These were 45 to 80 tons burden.

These round-bowed, narrow-pooped herring busses changed very slowly from one century to the next. With three masts setting square sails to the yards it was a much easier ship to sail. A main deck going right up to the bow and a high poop deck gave this vessel a distinctive look.

The design lasted up to the early 1700s and it is thought that the sail plan continued into the three-masted fishing lugger of between 1790 to the early 1800s. The name buss only applies to fishing vessels.

Fig 13.6A *An armed cutter. The type of sailing ship used by Revenue men to chase smugglers.*

Fig 13.6B *A bilander or billander (from the Dutch bijlander). A small European merchant ship of the 17th and 18th centuries used in the North Sea and more frequently to be found in the Mediterranean.*

Fig 13.7A A schooner with fore and aft sails on foremast and main. These ships originally carried square topsail on each mast. Later these were changed to jibheaded or jackyard topsails.

Fig 13.7B A brig. These were used widely for short and coastal trading voyages. Used in some navies as training ships for young sailors.

The Mayflower *1620*

A small merchant ship of the early 1600s. There are no official plans of this famous ship. Any models that have been built have relied heavily on those found in *Fragments of Ancient English Shipwrighting* of 1586 regarding the hull shape. Three masts, square-rigged with lateen sail on the mizzen.

Dutch and English warships 1670

Two deck men-of-war were developing in the late 1600s. The Dutch were prominent in this development.

The difference between the Dutch warship and the English was that the Dutch outboard planking on the poop and quarterdeck was clincher laid with only minor decoration. There were other variations between the Dutch and English vessels, particularly in their rigging.

English three-deck warships 1637

The first three-decker was commissioned in 1637. *Sovereign of the Seas* was not the success it was

Fig 13.8A A lugger used for fishing and coastal trading. The rig was developed in the late 17th and early 18th centuries. When working the tides these vessels had a great advantage over conventional square riggers. Privateers also found them a useful craft.

Fig 13.8B A snow was a two-masted merchant vessel and rigged as a brig. The name was used from the 16th to the 19th century. A very European ship not found anywhere else in the world.

Fig 13.9A *The ketch name covers a wide variety of craft built by the English, French and Dutch navies during the wars of the 17th and 18th centuries. They were adopted by the English who found them useful to mount their mortars on the reinforced decks.*

Fig 13.9B *An armed pinnace. This type of boat, originally a ship's boat, could be used for a number of different jobs in war. It could mount a small cannon in the bow and was used to land soldiers in raids on enemy coasts.*

Note: old prints published by Steel in 1818 for his book on rigging. They first appeared in Treatise on Naval Affairs *in the Royal Encyclopaedia 1791.*

hoped for. She was not very seaworthy and much overloaded with fancy carving.

Another famous ship was the *Prince* 1670. Some of the finest half dozen models of English lst Raters are still in existence today, including one of the *Prince* thanks to the habit of making a model when laying down a keel of ships in the mid-1600s.

Designed by Phineas Pett, she was launched at Chatham in 1670 and became the flagship of the Lord High Admiral of England (the Duke of York, afterwards James 11). *Prince* was broken up in 1692.

One feature of this ship that is important to note is the square tuck or transom stern, which had been introduced in the previous century and was now slowly being replaced by the round tuck in which the planking was curved around the stern quarter and carried into the rabbet of the sternpost.

Dutch yacht 1680

This is an important boat to mention in the evolution of sailing craft. These were extensively used in Holland where the development of the leeboard fitted both sides of the hull made these craft highly versatile sailing boats.

The early boats had rather cumbersome sprit sails like the Thames barge. By the middle of the century this had been discarded for a gaff rig holding the peak of the mainsail – this was sometimes curved making them instantly recognisable as Dutchmen. Charles II got to know these craft while in exile in Holland. He was so interested in this type of sailer that on returning to England he instructed leading shipwrights to design and build other yachts.

The king's brother also became interested and they both encouraged sailing contests between individual vessels, thus laying the foundation of yacht racing in England. The shipwrights soon discarded the Dutch hull design and based the new hulls on their own small 6th Rater men-of-war. The leeboard also went.

The twenty odd vessels mentioned above will give you a rough idea of some of the important ships over the centuries and establish the types of hull that continued to be developed in sailing boats up to the turn of this century.

There were many other like the 17th and 18th century English warships. Cook's *Endeavour*, a bark of 1768 is a good example of a commercial ship. She was an ex-Whitby collier.

The French men-of-war were considered by the British to be superior to their own ships and captured French vessels were soon put to use in the British fleet. It is an odd fact that the French crews had better ships but the crews were not as good as the English sailors who were highly trained in sea discipline and battle manoeuvres.

Some further names of craft to look for are listed below:

Corvette	Brig
East India merchantmen	Felucca
Ketch	Schooner
Frigate	Cutters
Xebec	Slavers
Luggers	Whalers

14 Sailing trawlers – old and new

If you are interested in old traditional fishing boats, look no further than the Brixham smack, one of the most widely known types of south-western fishing boats. In 1934 a man named Frank Carr identified over 200 distinct types of coastal working craft around our shores. The majority were fishing craft and most were locally built to suit the local conditions. Only a few are left today where enthusiasts have made the effort to preserve, and in some cases use, these interesting boats.

Brixham lies in the southern corner of Torbay, looking northwards. Well protected from the prevailing southwesterly gales, it is a good place to sail in and out of.

There are other types of sail-powered fishing smacks but my favourite is the Brixham boat.

The plan comes from a little book about these craft published in 1980, *Provident and the story of the Brixham smacks* by John Corin. The lines are from a boat built in 1924, see **Fig 14.4**.

The model graces the cover of this book. I made the hull from solid cedarwood, carving it from two pieces. The prow post, keel, rudder post and rudder were added after carving. The bulwarks and timberhead were added topside after the deck was laid. These were made from bought lime planks.

The dimensions of the original boat were as follows:

Fig 14.1 The hull of a Brixham trawler carved in cedarwood, with bulwarks and timberheads fitted topside after laying the deck.

Fig 14.1A & B The model ready for fitting the sails.

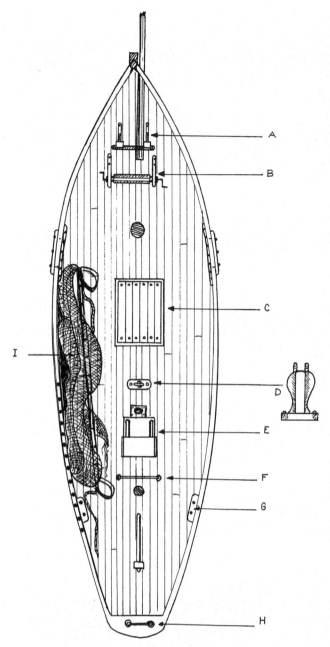

Fig 14.2 *Deck layout of Brixham trawler.*
A *Bitts*
B *Windlass*
C *Fish hold*
D *Pump head and towpost combined*
E *Hatchway to crew quarters with boiler plate and chimney on the foreside of the cabin*
F *Main sheet horse*
G *Mizzen shrouds to inside of bulwarks*
H *Mizzen sheet horse*
I *Trawlhead beam and net can be stowed on port side of deck.*
Note: The holes along the port top rail are for keeping the trawl main warp thole pin in place. The pin can be moved up or down the rail, depending on the warp angle needed.

Fig 14.3 *A Lowestoft drifter trawler.* **A** *General view of trawler.* **D** *Stern area of trawler showing mizzen stay sail and lifeboat with trawl net stowed.* **E** *Forward section of trawler showing fish hold covers and winch.*

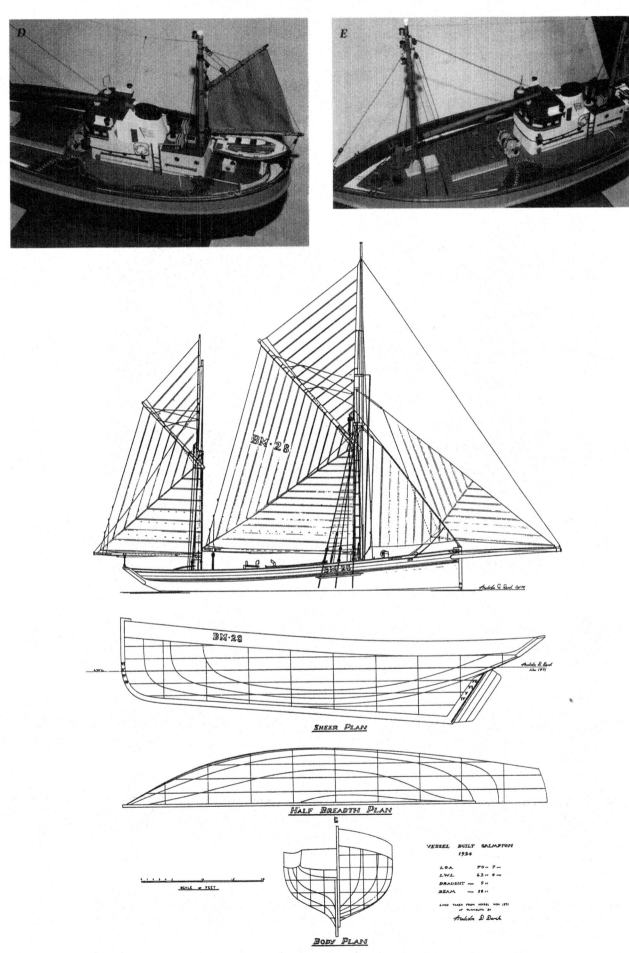

Fig 14.4 *A Brixham trawler plan. This was originally built in 1924.*

Fig 14.5 Brixham trawler 1925, the finished model on a stand.

- LOA 70ft 7in.
- LWL 62ft 4in.
- Draught max. 9ft
- Beam max 18ft

There is no deck detail shown on the plan but information from other sources has been used to finish off these details. See **Fig 14.2**, deck details.

The rigging is quite simple and the sails were homemade. The sail colour (reflecting the colour of the Devonshire soil!) was dyed into the material which was a white, thin calico. Tan-coloured material was impossible to find ready coloured.

I have put a waterline on the model. It is interesting to note the angle at which these boats sat in the water, reminiscent of some American working boats mentioned in this book.

There is a Nexus Plans Service sheet for a Brixham trawler No. MM 1275. The hull is 15¼in. long – 22in. overall length. My model, incidentally, is 21in. long overall.

A drifter trawler

Pictures of this carvel-built model are included for those readers interested in the more modern type of working boat. It is similar to those working out of Lowestoft and other east coast harbours. Nexus Plan No.1238 is similar to this model. Having quite roomy hulls they make excellent models to motorize should you be interested in taking to the water rather than having a static model.

Note the mizzen stay sail – these are rigged to help the steering and positioning of the boat at slow speeds. The trawler has a canoe stern. The fishing net was made from vegetable net bags from the greengrocer and the winches from bits and bobs from the scrapbox. The stand supports were made from some cast brass scrap, cut and polished.

There are a number of plans of the more modern working boats like this in the *Plans Handbook* (Nexus Special Interests) mentioned throughout this book.

Appendix A   Glossary of terms

Beam Breadth of ship at widest point.

Belaying pins These were made of wood or iron, truncheon shaped, tapering from the middle downwards and swelling towards the top. These push into pin racks, usually at chest height. The racks were joined to the inside of the bulwarks, slightly abaft each mast. Used for belaying light ropes to.

Bitts Usually a frame of two upright timbers with a cross-piece fastened horizontally near the head of uprights. Made of heavy square timber they were used to belay ropes and cables. Fore-gear and topsail sheet bitts are situated on the foredeck and round foremast. Other bitts are situated on different parts of the deck all of varying weights, depending on the degree of strength needed.

Blocks Made usually of wood consisting of two cheeks holding a pulley wheel (sheave) made of bronze or lignum vitae. Their use in ships was to increase mechanically the power of ropes. By threading multiple and single pulleys together various haul strengths are made.

Bluff bows Very rounded bows of some ships.

Bolster A piece of wood usually with a rounded edge fixed to the trestletree frame to prevent the chafing of the shroud lines around the mast.

Bolt rope A rope sewn to the edges of sails to finish and strengthen.

Bonnet An additional strip of sail that can be laced to the foot of main course or fore-and-aft sails to increase their driving efficiency.

Boom A spar at the foot of the main fore-and-aft sail. Minor booms were used to extend the square sail, these were attached to the main yards and called studding sail booms.

Bowsprit Stepped into or onto the bow, supported by shroud lines, bobstay and martingale lines, it supports the headsails of a ship.

Braces Attached to the ends of the yardarm to brace the sail around and trim the yard to the wind.

Bulkhead A vertical partition athwarthships, also for divisions fore and aft.

Bulwark The planking or woodwork wall along the side of a ship above the deck line.

Buttock The breadth of ship where the hull rounds down to the stern.

Caps Thick blocks of wood (later caps made of iron or steel) with two holes in them, used to confine the masts at the top end of the doubling area of mast. The space between the holes allowed room for the shroud ropes to pass between the two mast sections.

Carvel-built A type of side planking where the edges are fitted tightly together making a smooth finish. The joints are caulked.

Chainplates Thick iron rods or straps bolted to the sides of ships to which chains or shackles connect to the lower deadeye that support the masts' shrouds.

Channels Broad thick planks bolted edgeways against the ship's side through which the chainplates pass. This spaces the shrouds from each other.

Cheeks or bibbs Pieces of timber bolted to the mast on either side of a square-rigged ship to support the trestletrees.

Cleats Blocks of wood or metal shaped in various ways to belay ropes and lines to.

Clinker-built (Also clincher-built) A method of planking in which the lower edge of each plank overlaps the upper edge on the one below. A method normally used in small boat building.

Counter stern The overhang of the stern abaft the rudder.

Course The largest sails set upon all lower yards of a

square-rigged ship, referred to as fore course, main course etc.

Crab winch A hand winch positioned aft on either side of a barge, used to raise and lower leeboards etc.

Cringles Small rope loops on the sail bolt rope used to fasten different ropes including the leech rope.

Crosstrees(l) Part of the wooded frame running athwart of the mast that supports the tops.

Crosstrees(2) The word is sometimes used to describe both trestletrees and crosstrees which form a frame around the top mast and is left unboarded in this case.

Crotches Pieces of iron or wood shaped with a broad 'U' shaped top. They are usually mounted at deck level to support spare masts and yard timber.

Davit A stout boom fitted to the fore-channel, used to assist the lifting of the anchor keeping it clear of the ship's side. A kind of crane hoist, hinged on the channel. Also used to raise and lower the ship's boats, situated on the mizzen channels both sides. On the stern the Captain's gig was lowered on two davit arms permanently bolted in a horizontal position, projecting over the stern.

Deadeyes Wooden blocks, circular with flattened sides, pierced with three holes. A rope groove cut around the periphery. Used to reeve lanyards when setting up shrouds or stays.

Eye of a shroud The top end of a shroud formed into a served loop to go over the mast head.

Fid A large wooden or iron wedge that goes through the heel of the topmast. The fid rests on the trestletrees preventing the mast dropping through.

Forecastle deck Pronounced fo'c'sle – the forward deck and underpart.

Foremast The first mast mounted nearest to the bows of a square-rigged ship.

Freeboard The distance, measured in the centre of the ship, from waterline to deck level.

Frigate A class of three-masted warship, fully rigged on each mast. Armed with from 24 to 38 guns carried on a single gun deck. Rated 5th or 6th rate.

Futtock shroud The section of the shroud lines from the underside of the top that connect with the mast band in some cases, or the lower mast shrouds in others.

Gaffs A spar to which the head of a four-sided fore-and-aft sail is laced and hoisted on the after side of the mast.

Gammon lashing A rope lashing consisting of seven or eight turns passing or **gammoning** over the bowsprit and through a slot or hole in the stem. This was usually a cross lashing. Later in the 19th century it was replaced by a heavy metal band.

Gunwales The plank that covers the head of the timbers around the upper sheer strake of a ship.

Halyards, **Halliards** or **Haulyards** The cables or ropes used to hoist or lower sails and their yards. The heavy course sails (lowest sail on square-rigged ships) were hoisted by jeers from just under the tops.

Hammock nettings A stowage place for hammocks (bedding rolls of sailors). Old sailing warships had iron frames bolted to the sides of the centre section of deck and upper deck and along the break of the poop to act as protection from musket fire and wood splinters during battle. Capital ships had eight hundred odd men as crew so there were plenty of hammock rolls.

Hatch coamings Sturdy boards mounted vertically around deck openings like cargo hatches to prevent water running down into the openings. These were six to ten inches high in sailing ships with good freeboard but higher on seagoing barges.

Horses The rope that sailors stood on, slung under the yards of a square-rigged sail, when furling sails. A bowsprit horse runs parallel from the bowsprit and serves as a rail hold or foot rope for sailors going out on the bowsprit. Jib horses hang under the jib boom and are knotted into a course net as a safety foot net.

Hounds Wooden shoulders bolted below the masthead either side of some ships without trestletrees to support the shroud top.

Hull Body of the ship.

Jeers Heavy tackle consisting of double or treble blocks used for hoisting the lower yards in square-rigged ships. A jeer capstan was usually situated between fore and main masts to sway up the yards.

Jib boom This was an overlapped extension of the bowsprit held by a cap and band. This supported the fore topgallant and royal headstays and sails.

Keel The lowest and principal timber of a wooden ship running fore and aft.

King plank The centre plank of the ship's deck on wooden vessels.

King post A short mast close to cargo hatches from which is worked small cargo derrick.

Lanyards Short ropes threaded between deadeyes. Also to tie hearts together on main stays.

Leeboard An early type of drop keel made of wood pivoted outboard each side of barges and other flat-bottomed or shallow-draughted sailing vessels. Said to have been developed by the Dutch.

Lubber hole A small aperture in the top for the less brave to go through rather than climbing out via the futtock shrouds to gain the top.

Luff The leading edge of a fore-and-aft sail.

Lugsail A four-sided sail set on a lug or yard, used mainly in small craft.

Lutchet A similar fitting to the tabernacle at deck level found on spritsail barges or wherries allowing the mast to be lowered.

Main mast The centre mast of a square-rigged sailing ship.

Martingale A bar of wood, usually ash, projecting downwards from the underside of the bowsprit cap. The martingale stay supports the jib boom.

Mast A vertical spar set in a ship's deck to support other spars that in turn support the sails.

Mast butt The thick end of a mast nearest the keel, or thick end of masts above the lower mast.

Mizzen mast The name of the third, aftermost, mast of a square-rigged ship.

Mule rigged 'Mulie' mizzens, as on barges, consisted of a standard mizzen mast with conventional gaff and booms, as opposed to a sprit mizzen.

Parral A method of keeping a yard against the mast and to facilitate the swing, raising and lowering of the yard. Wooden trucks threaded on wooden ribs lashed around the mast.

Poop deck The stern or quarter deck.

Quoin A large wooden wedge used under the butt end of naval cannons to obtain elevation. Superseded later by various fast thread screws mounted to the gun.

Ratlings or **Ratlines** Small ropes that cross the shrouds horizontally at equal distances, forming a ladder to go up or down from the deck to masthead.

Running rigging Ropes and cordage, usually running on pulley blocks that control the sails and spars of sailing ships.

Scuppers These were draining holes or slots cut into the base of the deck bulwarks to drain surface water from the decks and waterways.

Sheave The revolving wheel in a block. Made of lignum vitae or brass.

Sheer Upward curve of deck towards bows and stern.

Sheets Any rope that controls a sail from its lower corners.

Ship draft Plans of ship.

Shipwrights The ship building experts.

Shrouds A variety of large ropes from the mastheads down to the sides of the ship, i.e. fore, main and mizzen shrouds. This also applies to the topmast shrouds. The bowsprit also has shrouds that support it.

Snotter Metal gear found on sprit-rigged vessels consisting of a ring collar which fits over the heel of the sprit boom. It is chain-linked to the metal main mast strap. This supports the sprit boom, holding it close to the mast.

Spar General term for timbers used in setting up the rigging and sails.

Spritsail A large fore-and-aft four-sided sail set on a sprit spar which stretched diagonally across the sail to support the peak. A typical barge rig. The name also describes a small square sail set on a yard beneath the bowsprit in a square-rigged ship, introduced in the 16th century.

Standing rig Stout rigging ropes which are permanently set up to support the masts of sailing ships, as in the shrouds.

Stay Part of the standing rigging of a sailing vessel which supports a mast in the fore-and-aft line. Forestays support forward and backstays from aft.

Stem The foremost timber of a ship. It is attached to the keel.

Sternpost The aftermost timber in the hull. It is attached to the keel and forms a fixing for the rudder.

Strakes Each line of planking in a wooden ship.

Swimhead bow Early type of barge bow, not unlike the wedge-shaped punt bow. Superseded by the straight stem bow.

Tabernacle A wooden or metal trunk fitted to the deck of sailing ships supporting the heel of a mast, stepped at deck level. A fitting usually found on vessels that have to lower masts under bridges.

Throat The inner end of a gaff or boom.

Timberheads Vertical timbers rising through deck affording fixings for bulwark planking.

Tops The platform structure fixed around the head of the lower mast that rests on the crosstrees.

Transom Stern bulkhead. The squared-off stern: sometimes vertical, often canted at an angle.

Trestletrees Part of the wooded frame, running fore-and-aft of the mast that supports the tops.

Truck A circular wooden cap with small sheaves fitted to the tops of masts. Used for signal flags. Can also refer to the wooden wheels of a gun carriage.

Tuck The shape of the afterbody of a ship under the stern or counter. The light fir-planked frigates built towards the end of the Napoleonic Wars (1803–15) had flat square transoms. They were known as square-tucked frigates.

Tumble home The amount by which the two sides of a ship are brought in towards the centreline after reaching their maximum beam.

Vang The two ropes leading from the outer end of a gaff in fore-and-aft sails to prevent leeward sagging of sail and give more control over gaff.

Wales An extra thickness of wood bolted to the sides of ships in positions where protection is needed.

Yards A large wooden spar crossing and attached to the mast horizontally to support a square sail.

A note on ships' colours

Around the early 1800s, naval hulls were black with yellow ochre bands as *HMS Victory*. The insides were originally red but later light yellow, ochre or broken white. Shortly after 1815 dark soft green was used for interiors and the external yellow or ochre bands became white.

Appendix B   Bibliography

Anderson, R. C. *Seventeenth Century Rigging* Model & Allied Publications 1972

Archibald, Michael *South Eastern Sail 1840–1940* David & Charles 1972

Campbell, G. F *Jackstay* Model Shipways Co. Inc. N.J.

Chappelle, Howard I. *American Sailing Craft* Bonanza Books NY

Chapelle, H. I. *The Search for Speed Under Sail* Geo. Allen & Unwin Ltd.

Chapman, F. H. *Architectura Navalis Mercatoria* Adlard Coles Ltd. 1768

Cooper, F. S. *Handbook of Sailing Barges* Adlard Coles Ltd. & John de Graff NY

Culver, Harry B. *Contemporary Scale Models of Vessels of the Seventeenth Century* Payson & Clarke NY 1926

Davis, C. G. *American Sailing Ships (Their Plans and History)* Dover Pub. Ltd. NY

Dudszus, Alfred & Henriot, Ernest *Dictionary of Ship Types* Conway Maritime Press 1986

Frere-Cook, Gervis (Ed) *The Decorative Arts of the Mariner* Jupiter 1974

Greenhill, Basil *The Archaeology of the Boat* A & C Black, London 1976

Greenhill, Basil & Gifford, Ann *Sailing Ships: Victorian & Edwardian from Old Photographs* Batsford Books

Haws, Duncan *Ships and the Sea* Hart Davis, MacGibbon, London 1976

Hazell, Martin *Sailing Barges* Shire Publications Ltd.

HMSO (Admiralty) *Manual of Seamanship* HMSO 1908 (revised 1915)

Hough, Richard *Fighting Ships* Michael Joseph 1969

Jobe, Joseph (Ed) *The Great Age of Sail* Edita Lausanne 1967

Jutsum, Capt. J. N. *Knots and Splices* The Nautical Press, Glasgow 1926

Kemp, Peter (Ed) *The Oxford Companion to Ships and* Oxford University Press, London, *the Sea* New York and Melbourne

Leavitt, John F. *Wake of the Coasters* The American Maritime Library vol. 2. 2nd ed 1984

MacGregor, David *Fast Sailing Ships 1775–1875* Conway 1988

MacGregor, David *Merchant Sailing Ships 1775–1815* Argus Books Ltd. 1980

McKee, E. *Working Boats of Britain* Conway Maritime Press 1983

Rees, Abraham *Rees's Naval Architecture 1816–20*

Slocum, Capt. Joshua, *Sailing Alone Around the World and Voyage of the Liberade*. Rupert-Hart-Davis 1948

Steel, David *Art of Rigging 1818* Fisher Nautical Press 1974

Van Powell, Nowland *The American Navies of the Revolutionary War* C.P. Putnam & Sons NY 1974

Various *Art and the Seafarer* Faber & Faber 1968

Various *The Law of Ships* Nordbook, Sweden 1975

Veryan, Heal *Britain's Maritime Heritage (Museums & Maritime Collections)* Conway Maritime Press

Williams, Guy R. *The World of Model Ships and Boats* Andre Deutsch 1971

Appendix C   Useful addresses

Maritime Models Greenwich
7 Nelson Road
Greenwich
London SE10

Tel: 0181 858 5661

For planking wood and all model parts etc., some plans.

Model Shipwright
International Quarterly Magazine
Conway Maritime Press Ltd.
101 Fleet Street
London EC4Y 1DE

Tel: 0171 583 2412

Nexus Special Interests
Plans Service
Consumer Division
Azalea Drive
Swanley
Kent BR8 8HU

Tel: 01322 660070

Euro Models
35 Crown Road
St Margarets
Twickenham
TW1 3EJ

Tel: 0181 891 0342

No plans except with kits. All materials needed for model ships made from scratch.

Brown Son & Ferguson
4–10 Darnley Street
Glasgow G412 S10

Tel: 0141 429 1234

The publishers of all Harold A. Underhill ship plans.

David R. MacGregor
12 Upper Oldfield Park
Bath BA5 3JZ

No phone calls, letters only. For plans of many interesting old ships.

National Maritime Museum
Romney Road
Greenwich
London SE10 9NF

Tel: 0181 858 4422 (general information)
0181 855 1647 (plans department)

Other titles of interest from Nexus Special Interests

Model Ships from Scratch
Scott Robertson

In this first title, Scott Robertson shows you how you can build an end product of fascination, history, skill and value using low-cost materials and a minimum of tools from scratch. The text is packed with useful hints and tips which, together with a number of detailed drawings and photographs, provides a very practical guide to the art and craft of model ship building.

1994, ISBN 1-85486-105-0, 160 pages + 4pp colour plates, A4 paperback

The Period Ship Handbook
Keith Julier

Have you ever been put off by the thought of all that planking and rigging? This book helps the beginner and the more experienced alike to overcome some of the real, and the mythical, problems of model ship construction. Using a number of commercially available kits as a basis for discussion, the book provides detailed, step-by-step procedures for making each model. Invaluable for beginners and all modelmakers with an interest in building period ship models without the need for sophisticated workshop facilities.

1992, ISBN 1-85486-081-X, 208 pages + 4pp colour plates, A4 paperback

The Period Ship Handbook 2
Keith Julier

A further venture into the world of static model sailing ships, offering guidance to the beginner and discussion on modelmaking for the more experienced. Suggestions on expanding the tool kit from the basic essentials towards more sophisticated equipment are followed by an overall view of commercially available kits and their selection. The main body of the book is devoted to the building of ten models, all available in kit form. Each vessel selected has something different to offer the modelmaker, whether it be ornamentation or miniature authentic carpentry. Information is provided on the English Rate system and the book concludes with a summary of more modelling techniques.

1995, ISBN 1-85486-132-8, 144 pages + 4pp colour plates, A4 paperback

The titles listed above should be available from all good bookshops.
In the event of difficulty, please contact
Nexus Special Interests, Books Division, Nexus House, Azalea Drive, Swanley, Kent BR8 8HU.
Tel: 01322 660070.

NOTES

NOTES

NOTES

NOTES